Change In My Pocket

Rebeca Books
The 1C Story Network
933 Creech Rd #8
Naples, FL 34103
Rebecabooks.com

Rebeca Books is the publishing division of The 1C Story Network.

The publisher is not responsible for websites (or their content) that are not owned by the publisher.

The 1C Speakers Bureau provides a wide range of content creators, experts, authors, and more for speaking events. To find out more, visit justonec.com or call (407) 490-2690.

Library of Congress Control Number:
Due to the shutdown of the U.S. Government at time of printing, the Library of Congress ceased to function. To receive current information about this title's inclusion in the Library of Congress, please contact Rebeca Books at (407) 490-2690 or rebeca@rebecabooks.com.

Tradepaper ISBN
978-0-9970642-7-8

9 8 7 6 5 4 3 2 1

1st edition, January 2026

Typeset by The Book Typesetters
thebooktypesetters.com

Praise for *Change In My Pocket*

Finally! A stellar guide to navigating life's financial pivot points, from a woman who knows change firsthand and has led countless clients through it. With women on track to control 67% of wealth by 2030, this book arrives right on time.
Shannon Spotswood, CEO, RFG Advisory and Former Hedge Fund Manager

As long as I have known Shari, she has been interested in more than the bottom line. She has a passion for helping people meet their financial goals so that they may fulfill their sense of mission and purpose. She sees change not merely as a disruption, but as an opportunity. It's our Choice.
Travis Collins, PhD, Senior Pastor of First Baptist Church of Huntsville

Shari uniquely blends nakedly honest autobiography with sound, pragmatic advice for navigating change. It is a very compelling approach that resonates.
Rex Geveden, President and CEO, BWXT

It was a quick read with prompts for easy introspection to embrace change as possibility and not a detour. Her tools help you define specifics of what will be meaningful and fulfilling in whatever your next chapter holds ... with guardrails for sound financial advice along the way...
Cynthia Lassiter, MD—OBGYN, Henderson and Walton Women's Center

Change In My Pocket offers clarity, guidance and most of all HOPE to women navigating life changes. As a divorced, triplet mom who has changed careers, I wish someone had given me a copy of this book! I will definitely gift it to friends facing big change in the future.

Lisa Greer Morris, Partner at Greer Investments

Shari is a gifted writer. I've read countless self-help books, but none have struck the heart of the matter quite like this one. Her personal story drew me in immediately—I felt as if I were having coffee with a wise, trusted friend who cuts through the noise to deliver solid counsel for life's hardest moments. My only regret is not having this book 30 or 40 years ago. Still, I'm deeply grateful it came into my life now. A refreshing, timely guide for facing change and loss with strength and clarity. One of a kind.

Lynn Phillips-Gaines, Founder, Phillips Wealth Planners

Change In My Pocket

Your Purse-Sized Guide to Navigating Change Now

by Shari Moxley

Contents

ACTIONS IN THE FACE OF CHANGE

Foreword

I f you've opened this book, chances are high that you're facing change, and you probably have some feelings about that. As a woman in my fifties with more than thirty-five years of service as a financial advisor, I've both experienced and observed an incredible amount of change.

Perhaps there's been a death and you're facing the looming task of managing the enormity of what you and your partner built together. Or maybe you looked around, saw the depth and breadth of what you've built on your own—and realized that it's time to transition into some version of retirement. It could be as simple as recognizing the complexity of life in the stage you're in and knowing some sort of change is needed, and soon. Perchance it's something else entirely.

Regardless, I'll bet you've opened this book because a change is afoot in your life.

While it may feel foreign and new and scary to you at present, change itself is actually a pretty predictable phenomenon. It possesses characteristics of its own, and a set of actions exist that are effective in moving through it. Because I've spent decades helping people navigate change from the perspective of getting not only themselves but also their loved ones, interests, and wealth through it intact, I've been privy to a steady, observable seat in the phenomenon of change.

What you're about to read is not the end of a developing body of knowledge about managing change within our lives. It's simply what I've learned until this point. I provide it here because I believe if we don't share our stories and wisdom with each other, we lose the ability to expand upon them and keep progressing as a society. We end up starting at square one over and over again. We settle into a place of perpetual stagnation.

And, as you're about to read, stagnation is the very last thing my lived story could ever come to terms with. As a matter of fact, I don't think any of us gets out of here without encountering change.

Here's your permission to stuff this little book in your purse or keep it handy by the bedside table for a few weeks as you make your way through your change. I hope you emerge from your time in these words with additional understanding, knowledge, and insight as you choose to make change the solution and not the problem.

So, in the interests of helping you not only survive change, but thrive in its aftermath, let's go on a 21-day journey together...

1

Origin Story

Change [cheynj]
verb
to make the form, nature, content, future course, etc., of (something)
different from what it is or from what it would be if left alone

Looking back, I think I must have been destined to live within the throes of change. Born on a clear, crisp February day in Savannah, Georgia, to Lydia and Larry, I literally didn't have my feet beneath me before the first change arrived. At six months old, Lydia and Larry relocated us to Jacksonville, Florida—a change of venue to chase the American Dream of a better job and a better life. Formal education began there in what Mom later laughingly called a "lily white, Presbyterian" school. Nobody was rich. Nobody was poor. Everybody was comfortable.

Pretty auspicious start to life, right?

Ah, but change. She never lurks too long in the shadows before waltzing back into my life.

It turns out, my father wasn't as comfortable as the

outward picture indicated. A basketball and baseball star in high school, he played for the farm team of the Cleveland Indians for a while but couldn't punch through to the Big Show. That inability to embrace a change in plan delivered a massive blow to his ego. He couldn't achieve his real dream, so he went into finance and sales as a stock broker with Merrill Lynch. There, he found not only a career with bonuses that afforded him the ability to buy a new car, he also discovered wine and women.

I was five when he and my mother divorced. Mom continued on in her work as the assistant to the president of the local junior college and, as she later told me, kept going some days solely because she had a daughter to provide for.

I think sometimes about the differences in my parents' reactions to change. One pivoted to a different career path but left behind the discipline and self-governance that his previous dream required. In doing so, he made destructive choices. The other got hit by the change wave, held her breath until she could get above water, gulped in a lungful of air, and kept swimming through the storm. She made different choices for her own preservation.

After Mom and I found my father in a lie and deep in an affair, Mom filed for divorce and didn't want much to do with men thereafter. She had enough on her hands with keeping the two of us above poverty in the wake of the last man. But the summer she separated from my father, a man walked into Mom's office named Rob. Where Larry was handsome, Rob was persistent. He put his excellent conversational skills to work, swooping into the coffee pot area next to Mom's office and going after what interested him: her.

She said it was the sound of his voice that kept her interested.

Perhaps it was the deep waters within him that settled her.

I was 7 years old when Mom married Rob, the man who adopted me and became "Dad." In our family, we always say "we" got married, and it really was like that. The three of us formed our own little unit as we left Jacksonville, Florida for Norfolk, Virginia.

Dad's family didn't initially love his addition of a divorced woman with a daughter to the family, so only the three of us celebrated birthdays and holidays in those first few years. And that was okay. Honestly, their choice of withdrawal in the face of change didn't dawn on me until much later in life. At the time, I focused on being a good daughter and a good student in this new school whose student body was so much more colorful than the one I'd left behind.

Dad was the first one who told me, "You can do anything."

And I actually believed him.

Dad's career aspiration was to be a college president. That meant change. Lots of it. To climb the college ladder, one must move from college to college, reaching a higher rung each time. Most cities only have one college, so moving from one to another requires changing cities. We lasted two years in Norfolk with Dad at Old Dominion University before packing up and heading off to Atlanta.

I did a lot of growing up in the city of peaches, Southern drawls, and "Bless your heart." Running track and cross country—often training with Dad on runs—gave both structure and community to those days. (I never went fast, I could just go long. Must've gotten it from my mom, the queen of staying the course even if meant running a marathon.) My innate desire for approval motivated a string of straight A's and sports achievements as I progressed toward the upper echelon of our K-8 school. Four years in, though, another rung on his corporate ladder presented itself to Dad.

For the first time, the wave of change hit me hard. It was much harder than previous changes. I'd begun to dig some roots into the soil of friendships. Established myself. In our other locations, I'd had friends at school or next door, but in Atlanta I would go to my girlfriends' houses and play and vice-versa. These were friends *on purpose,* not chosen solely for geographic convenience but because we truly enjoyed being in each other's company. I even had a boyfriend! Ah, first crush.

When Mom and Dad sat me down and said we were moving, I didn't exactly take it lightly. This was the first time I didn't feel like I was merely being pulled up and headed off to a new experience with barely a goodbye. No, this time I would be leaving connections I'd invested with abandon. I'd even managed to get onto the school dance team! How could I leave behind this emblem of being at least somewhat good at being a girl, with its fun moves and flirty skirt uniform especially since I wasn't coordinated enough to make the cheerleading squad? Smack in the face. All that progress gets to be blown up with yet another move and another series of change.

See, the thing about change is that it often does not show up accompanied by the options of denying or arguing its arrival. Change doesn't pause or peek through the door opening and say, "If you don't want me here, I'll go." No, it blows through the door and it's there, taking up space in your living room, whether you want it or not.

So, when Mom and Dad told me we were leaving Atlanta and heading to Richmond, I repeated the mantra that has served me well ever since.

"Well, gotta do it again." Just with a lot more door slamming, foot stomping, rolling eyes, and tears.

Richmond turned out to be a two-year stint before we packed up again and headed off to Birmingham, Alabama, for Dad to serve as the vice president of Birmingham Southern College. He oversaw finance, operations, security, and the athletic program. With this move, Dad said the magical words, "We're done. No more moves." Lucky me! I'd get to spend all four years at Vestavia High School. Go, Rebels!

Using skills I'd honed back in Atlanta, I formed friendships and got involved quickly. I lived at my grandparent's house... the ones who weren't happy with Dad's marital decision... to help get me established in a strong school district until a smart house purchase in the area could materialize. Being a Southern belle herself, Sue-Sue felt it her grandmotherly duty to send me to charm school and encourage me to branch out beyond my go-to athletic extracurricular activities. I delved back into cross-country and track and, because of her influence, I added theater, voice lessons, choirs, and even a few beauty pageants (the ones which favored the smart girls). Even that charm school choice didn't go to waste; I was elected to be one of the high school hostesses (Go Rebel Girls!) and got into student government. Funny, it seemed like all that activity landed me at the top of the "B" team or in the play's chorus, never the star or winner, which was fine with me because being a student seemed to be my greatest strength.

By the time high school graduation rolled around, I'd had:

- Two dads
- Seven homes
- Six cities

And a whole lot of trying new things to adapt.

That's quite a bit of upheaval for 18 years of life, so the thought of moving away for college didn't phase me in the slightest. I held every intention of packing up my well-used suitcases and heading off to either an Ivy League college (for my smart side) or The University of Alabama (for my now developing social side). That is... until I caught sight of a very, very pretty boy in a very, very pink button-down shirt on the campus of Birmingham Southern College at a prospective college student weekend. (Hi, Robbie Tapscott. This is probably news to you.) Who's to say I couldn't hold fast to Mom's, "Education is everything," directive *and* date a hot frat boy?

Suddenly, the thought of staying in Birmingham seemed like a mighty fine idea.

I moved into a dorm on the campus over which my father held such authority, declared Business and English as my major and minor, respectively, and set about equipping myself to earn a good living upon graduation.

Four years later, they handed me a Bachelor of Arts and, right on the heels of that, I also earned my MRS degree by marrying *not* the boy in the pink button-down but Bo, a different handsome young man who was adept at conversation. I then set out on a career as a financial advisor—a job that literally navigates change every second of every day.

After all the upheaval of early life, I'd managed to stay in one city for a full eight years. Ninety-six months. Four hundred sixteen weeks. I'd never been in one place so long!

But, I'm a soul destined to live in the throes of change.

So are you, really. We all are. Even if you've lived in the same town your entire life and been married to the same man for fifty years, I bet you often define the phases of your life by change.

"Oh, that was before we got married."

"Oh, that was before we bought the house."

"Oh, that was after we had the kids."

"That was after I took that job."

"That was after I got laid off."

"That was after I retired."

You order the story of your life by its change points.

Some come into those change points kicking and screaming, filled with indignation or dread or anything but acceptance. You might be staring a change down right now, mired in those kinds of feelings. Even if you're not, though, you've been on the planet long enough to know that another change is inevitably coming. Change is life.

So, what if you had some insight for navigating the path when it twists with change?

And what if that wisdom came from a woman who not

only has managed her own changes since birth and her clients' changes for decades, but also learned to do so in a way that *benefits* life and its bottom line?

You're holding that navigation guide in your hand right now.

In thirty-five years of work as a financial advisor, I've come to see that change is nothing to fear. As a matter of fact, it can be a catalyst for growth on all sort of levels from financial to psychological, relational to spiritual. Countless hours in my office with clients have exposed me to hundreds of stories of change. Birth. Death. Divorce. Marriage. Business start. Business end. Life philosophy shift. Natural disasters. Decline of health. Devastating diagnoses. Relocations. You name it, and I've likely helped a client navigate it and even find the benefit within it.

Now that you know a little bit more about me, I hope you'll let me help you find the benefit within your change, too.

Let's start with getting to know change as an entity unto itself.

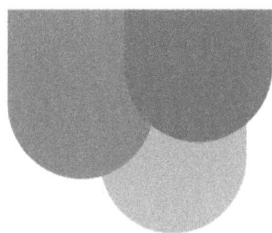

THE
CHARACTERISTICS
OF CHANGE

2

Your Approach to Change Determines Its Effect

"Any life is a life of change... If you can learn to cope with change, you'll lower your risk for anxiety and depression. Your relationships will flourish, and your body will feel healthier. But if you can't cope with change, only a minor amount of stress can make you feel overwhelmed by life."

Kathleen Smith, Ph.D., LPC

Your approach to change determines its effect in your life.

Read that again.

No, you cannot completely control whether and what changes will enter your life, and you've likely learned that by now. But here's the thing: If you choose to approach change as an opportunity to learn and examine toward a better result, you become able to address what comes your way and make real progress through it.

Change does not mean that all of your choices have

been ripped away. I tell you this from a place steeped in decades of navigating change for myself and alongside my clients. The key to long-term happiness, joy, and fulfillment lies in you embracing that you *do* have choices, even if they aren't quite apparent in your present circumstances.

Look around and find your choices *within* the changes.

When my mom and I discovered that my dad was cheating on that long-ago chilly Halloween day in Jacksonville, we still had choices. We could choose to live in reactionary anger and bitterness for the remainder of our time on earth. Each of us could have chosen to let that discovery become the defining moment of our lives.

Or, we could live within the pain of it for a time, look for lessons, and let it change us only so far as it made us better humans for the next part of the journey.

We could choose to abandon him entirely, never speaking to or about him again.

Or, we could find a way to maintain contact with someone who had been instrumental in our lives to that point while putting boundaries in place in the relationship to usher in an emotionally healthy future.

Mom could have chosen to never love a man again.

I could have chosen to never trust a man.

Or we could choose to not extrapolate one man's actions onto an entire half of the human species.

You, too, have choices within the change. They are life's gifts to you. Open those gifts with curiosity and wonder. A more fulfilled existence can be possible because choices exist in almost every circumstance. Your primary choices in the face of change are:

1. How will I react to this?
2. What will be different about me as a result of this?

There is a path to create a unique "better you," no matter the situation you find yourself in today. Embracing this time to make a change, make choices, and make new memories is possible and will be more rewarding with your openness to a few basic ideas. Embracing this characteristic of change—that it has inherent choice—starts with a few simple tenets.

Choose to Re-learn. Whatever changes you have experienced may lead to something very new. This means old habits or ideas may or may not move with you into your new present. A mind open to new ways can be the catalyst for stepping through the change.

Choose to Re-Look. Now is your opportunity to shake things up a bit. You're free to find new opportunities now, either by creating them or pursuing an existing one differently. Look hard. Brainstorm. Assume that what you see isn't the complete picture.

Choose to Re-Prioritize. What were your core values, personally and professionally, before this change? Are they the same or do you want to change them? You can. You're in charge of you and can decide to be a different you. What is important to you, *now*? How do you want to spend your time from this point forward? It's fine if you choose to keep some elements the same, of course. Just be sure you've *chosen*.

Choose to Re-Plan. What would your life look like with new goals? What are your plans for the next one, five, or ten years? Have you or should you release former dreams or pursuits? Conversely, should you become even more dedicated to them in the wake of this? Your unique change allows you multiple options to explore directions that were once off the table. Keep in mind that exploration takes time, so afford yourself some grace here.

Choose to Re-Cover. Your normal is over. Even if, once this change passes, your life resumes its previous patterns, *you* are changed by this change. There is no total return to the way it was before. Give your mind, body, spirit, and soul the time they need to adapt to this truth. Maybe you only need an hour. Maybe you need a year. It's your choice. Take the time it takes.

We'll unpack many of these together in the coming days. For now, I'd like you to spend the remainder of today thinking about the change that brought you to this book. Rather than focusing on what it is taking, can you hone in on the choices it has brought to your table?

3

Change Offers the Chance to Practice Adaptability

Adaptability [*uh*-dap-*tuh*-bil-i-tee]

noun

An individual's ability to adjust to new conditions, situations, or challenges flexibly and proactively

I sat in my office with a new client who had a furrowed brow and confusion in her eyes.

"Is this really all there is?" she asked me.

She'd reached her goal: retirement. Her financial needs were met for the remainder of her life and she was finally free to set work down.

This client is not alone with her question. Here in the United States, we've been infused with the idea of working for a number of years so that we can retire and live blissfully. Retirement has come to represent a happy life.

But that's as big a misunderstanding as the idea that reaching a particular financial goal equals a happy life.

"Once I have no debt, I'll live my happy life."

"Once I own my property free and clear, I'll live my happy life."

"Once I have a few million in the bank, I'll live my happy life."

"Once I sell this business, I'll live my happy life."

"Once I retire, I'll live my happy life."

None of these are true. And why is that?

The answer lies right outside your window. It's in the changing landscape. The grains of dirt being moved around by the ants. The snow falling or blades of grass working their way up, up, up. It's in the car driving down the road. The breeze moving dandelion seeds through the air.

Life *is* adaptation. Put another way: life *is* change.

It's right there in the way you remodeled your house after that last child moved out. Or how you switched your hair color (or stopped switching it). It's in that moment of opening a new credit card or closing one. Staying in the stock market or hopping out of it. Contributing to your 401k or withdrawing from it.

To live is to adapt.

You were created to grow and mature as part of the natural cycles of life. We accept the ongoing progression of change in the skies, the weather, or other animal life, yet we fight it as something unnatural for ourselves. Funny, isn't it? You'd never question that the clouds shift, or the animals move toward the food, or the plants climb toward the sun, but for some reason you question change's place within your own existence. After years of walking out life with my clients, I've come to think that we humans see change as a fixed moment instead of experiencing it in its true nature: a series of incremental shifts that lead to recognizable changes, culminating in an entire life story.

Beyond that, there's another truth that becomes apparent after years of helping people navigate change: the struggle is part of the adaptation process. Did you know a caterpillar has to *completely dissolve its own body* within the cocoon before it begins becoming a butterfly? Talk about a struggle! But the next phase of its life can't start until it completely exits the previous phase.

Action is taken when present pain outweighs the anticipation of future pain. (Good quote, Dad!)

Are you someone who thinks, "I can't change" often? Well (and please hear this with the gentleness and Southern lilt in which it is delivered), you're wrong, darlin'.

Consider all the changes you've already made. You learned to walk. Talk. Feed yourself. Drive. Get a job. Love. Be loved. Maybe have children or choose to not have children. Learn. Do math. Read. Gain weight. Lose weight. Walk in heels. Put your hair up. Take your hair down. Apply mascara. Choose not to apply mascara. When you really start to think about it, you've made a *ton* of changes. Clearly, you *can* change. You were born with the ability to adapt.

If you've ever visited a lake in the humid South, you've likely seen a cypress tree. They're the ones with the knobby "knees" all around the trunk base. They take up to forty years to mature and, to get there, they've had to learn to adapt within their flood-prone areas. A cypress tree has a shallow root structure. Now, what do you think happens if your roots aren't far down and the top layer of soil becomes flooded? You guessed it—you fall over.

But not the cypress tree.

He's *adapted*. Those knobby knees trap more soil around its hundred-foot height. They're like additional hands holding down the soil when the water comes to loosen it. So, the wind can come, and the temperatures can plummet and soar, but ole knobby-kneed cypress has adapted to endure.

You can, too. (And you can hide your knobby knees in a killer pair of slacks, if you so choose.)

I love how being in nature grounds me and heals me. It returns me to my senses and reminds me how life works.

Do you remember the last time you took a leisurely walk? Did you take a deep breath, look up at the sky, close your eyes, and let the sun hit your face? Do it! In that moment, your body begins to respond to the environmental change. You'll become aware of the light and warmth. The cadence of your breath will likely shift. Your heartbeat will slow. Your entire neurological function recalibrates. Within that moment, it is possible to redirect your focus inward, upward, or beyond the stressor on which you were initially focused. In that moment, it is possible to feel comfort and protection. Choose to participate in your immediate surroundings and give yourself the gift of a temporary metamorphosis.

You are connected to this earth in ways science tries repeatedly to explain, but still lacks the complete vocabulary for. Celebrating your place among all of nature helps unlock your ability to adapt to the changing circumstances of life. After all, there are rainbows after the rain. The sun does shine after a storm. And flowers do bloom in the spring, no matter how much snow came the season before.

You, too, can bloom from the deep, dark, rich soil of your change.

You *can* adapt because you were *created* to adapt. It's how you grow. How you become a better you.

We're going to work on that together in the coming days. For the remainder of today, allow yourself to enjoy and even anticipate that you have been given an opportunity to adapt and find new life.

4

Not All Change Is Equal, But All Change Passes

"Death is not the opposite of life, but a part of it."

Haruki Murakami

"Look, Shari, I'll buy that we can choose how we respond to change and that we're born to adapt," you might say, "but there's a difference between changing my hair color or the layout of my house and burying my husband, parent, or child."

And you are, of course, right.

Some changes leave broken pieces in their wake. And, sometimes, you're one of those pieces.

People living in the South (like me) know all about tornadoes. You live with them as a natural part of life. I've now added a home in Florida to my life, so I'm also learning all about hurricanes. For both of these forces of nature, the immediate experience of chaotic wind and rain can be present for mere seconds or minutes.

But the wake?

Oh, it's a mess of destruction. Pieces of people's lives are left scattered. An overturned car here, a worn family photo album there. Sterling flatware faithfully polished for generations ends up nearly unidentifiable within the rubble. The flood of water climbs its way up walls that were painted and papered by loving hands. Homes crumble. Entire towns get leveled.

It's hard not to wonder if it's even possible to move forward with all the mess.

The wake of a tornado or hurricane is, for me, a good visual representation of what happens inside us when someone we love dies. Everything gets ripped up, thrown around, and left in jagged edges that make it hurt to breathe. Outwardly, the clothes and carefully curated belongings of the person remain and must be managed. The rooms still smell like them. The memories come fast and furious as you enter stores and restaurants you both enjoyed.

It's devastating to move from making memories to being left with them.

I know.

I hear you.

Grief is such an unbearable pain that standing still may be the only choice we can make.

And that's okay, for a time.

To get through that time, I found it helpful to remind myself that death, too, brings me a choice. I can choose to die as well, or to live. In living, I can make all sorts of choices that might be different now that I'm living without the physical presence of the person I love.

Maybe I choose to sleep in the middle of the bed now. Maybe I decide to point my investments only toward companies whose values align with mine. Maybe I travel to places solely because they interest me. Maybe I get a different vehicle. Maybe I pour my heart into a different venture altogether because now the decision is mine alone.

The life I build after the burial is mine to choose.

Yours is yours to choose.

Take your time. It's going to pass whether you allow it to or not, so you may as well use that passage to your advantage. Rest within it. Remember within it. Grieve within it. Choose within it. Build anew within it.

The crushing change of death is rooted within that defiant feeling inside of you—the one that says you cannot accept this. It claims you cannot move forward, that there is nothing left for you in the face of this death.

But remember what's happening right outside your window. Change, change, change. It's all always changing. Life means change. Death is a part of the change. Death proves life was present.

For me, time moved the sharp pain of death's loss first into an ever-present fog which eventually moved into a catalyst of gentle remembrance. From within the place of my new life, I am able to smile at or at least appreciate the good things that are left behind—from that first big loss. It's like there is a type of gratitude for having known him— flaws and all—even though I spent much of life without his presence.

As it turns out, my biological father was an alcoholic. He struggled with the addiction his whole life. As I met his third wife and her family for the first time after his funeral,

I didn't feel completely at home (never being asked to meet), and yet I didn't feel like an outsider. I just assumed an alcoholic wouldn't be good to most anybody, and I found nothing could be further from the truth. Larry had met a woman, the widow of a minister, who loved him and could look past the times he would fall off the wagon. Her family seemed to embrace him too. In childhood, I prayed that my dad wouldn't die alone in a gutter. My prayers were answered. And I no longer feel sorry for him and the choices he made. Sometimes we get caught up in the act of agreeing or disagreeing with people's choices, and it keeps us from interacting with them or being able to enjoy their company. That doesn't mean that person has no worth or value as a human, and I can't see a world where God would allow someone to exist and not use something for some good purpose. There was beauty in his brokenness. His death put an end to an addiction, but also to all the closeness he felt with his wife and those around him.

Two decades after my father's funeral, as I grappled with a second divorce of my own, I took off for a long weekend at a nearby monastery for some alone time. On one of the walks around the grounds, I saw an old tossed-out window with a dirty, busted pane lying in the surrounding woods. How odd that the monks wouldn't have cleaned up old junk like that, I thought. I went over to pick it up and properly dispose of it, or at least hide it deeper in the woods to preserve the beauty of this little nature walk. I stopped dead in my tracks. A rush of chills raced across my whole body. The opposite of a hot flash, but just as intense, and it took the breath right out of me. The window pane was indeed broken by a rock and splintered to the point it rendered the window useless for its original purpose. It will probably stand as one of my life's most amazing examples of natural art. From the crack of the rock that hit the glass, the pane splintered in a perfect picture: a hummingbird in the sunlight. Surely my eyes weren't the only ones to see this little jewel.

I sat silent for a while. Why was I meant to find this? *Beauty out of brokenness.* Another cold rush. As broken as my marriage had become, I realized I was still capable of providing some beauty and goodness. So it was for Larry as well. Choices. All choices. Goodness can come from our pain and sorrow.

Finding my way into new life was aided by formulating a plan. Planning won't solve all your problems, of course, but it provides a blueprint for how to pick up the pieces and build again. No one's grief looks the same, and no two plans are the same. Yours might have step one as grief counseling, step two as transitioning out of your job, step three as selling your property and traveling the world. Or yours could include returning to your work or developing a new hobby. You've got options.

Your plan to transition from the life you knew before the death to the one you're building in its wake will be specific to you. Make it. Get an advisor to help if that helps you. Then, stick with it.

One day, you, too, will be in a place where your memories serve as a gift of joy and richness and proof of your ongoing life well lived. They'll become milestones on the long road you're meant to travel.

This change, too, will pass. And you have choices.

5

Change Brings New Faces and Places

"Old friends pass away, new friends appear. It is just like the days. An old day passes, a new day arrives..."

Dalai Lama

Another characteristic of change is that it brings along the introduction of new faces and places into life.

In my early twenties, I began working under the umbrella of a company in Alabama we'll call GreenRock that focused mainly on banking and related services. They brought me on board because I knew wealth management and could offer them a substantial revenue-generating financial service for their banking clients. They were early adopters to the concept that banks could provide more than CDs and savings accounts, but there were few roadmaps to follow in rolling out a program of this nature to such a huge client base. I was hired to assist in the change. And in the beginning, everything went well. They did their thing. I did mine. Clients were happy. The company accomplished its goal of launching a new service line. Everyone was happy.

But then a prospective client asked *me* for investment advice instead of the person at the company with whom he'd worked a few years earlier—an interaction that he did not immediately disclose to me. Now, to be clear, he'd barely had any contact with that other person. No relationship or ongoing communication or portfolio management. He'd been offered a product in which to invest his settlement money. He purchased it. That was that. Five years passed. In that five years, we met and he began talking to me about how much it was going to take to retire.

We opened a few accounts and were on our way to him retiring in five to seven years. Because I had a more advice-based relationship with him, I began to learn more and more about his entire life and goals. He was really tight-lipped early in our interactions, and the more time passed, the more I learned about the assets he was holding back from the discussion.

And that, my friend, is how I got myself fired from GreenRock, a company that had a policy of not allowing crossover of clients within the organization (which spanned over 15 locations at the time).

I stand by my decision then. I did what served the client, not the company, and—so long as I'm laying down my truths here, I'll set this down, too—I'd do it again.

That choice, though, brought change into my life on a timetable I did *not* choose.

This eventually taught me a lesson that I'll pass on to

you: Expect that change will open the door for new people and places to enter your life. Welcome that newness instead of fighting it.

Following through on a plan I'd been working for six months, I moved my business dealings beneath the umbrella of Raymond James Financial Services which was, at the time, one of the largest independent financial services firms. There, I met Kathy from Clarksville, TN—who has been one of my best friends ever since. She and I were two of the first women financial advisors in the room back at the turn of the century (literally, it was 2000). Kathy is the yin to my yang. The calm rock to my tempest. The steady, even-keeled boat to my dancing, frothing waves. She's empathetic, authentic, steadfast, and a truly incredible friend.

When I think about how I could've missed having her in my life if I'd fought to stay at GreenRock, my breath goes.

A beautiful life is one that incorporates new people! Newness is an opportunity, not a threat. It's a chance to indulge in curiosity, to be inquisitive. And if your new people (like my Greenrock manager, of sorts) don't exactly jive with you—or see you as a threat (sometimes we strong women get that rap), well just realize the importance of finding something to live with and agree on. Great relationships—or even tolerable ones—are built on finding just one piece of common ground.

The closing of one chapter can be the opening of another. Don't feel intimidated by the introduction of newness. As much as you'd prefer some situations to remain the same, they simply can't. Remember—your time, ideas, insights, and life are constantly moving. You close off your options when you are against seeing what could be on the other side of change.

In doing all this meeting of new people and considering new ways, you're going to need to exercise patience. (I know, I know.) You can't understand what you don't know, though, right? And knowing takes time. Finding common ground with someone can take time.

I counsel people on investments pretty much all day every day. Investment isn't only about money, though. It's also about time—investing time into new places and meeting new people, finding common ground, and building relationships. It's a *choice*.

I chose to invest time into my new place and the new people I encountered there.

As a result, I gained an incredible close friend, clients who are interesting and let us serve them every day, and work that earned me national recognition[1].

Forcing change—or choosing it—isn't always what brings new faces or new places into our lives. Sometimes change just gets dumped on us, and even good planning sometimes goes awry. Bringing families together isn't easy. I guess that's why choosing trustees and successor trustees with assets is an exercise best done with a lot of thought. I vividly recall a client who lost her new husband to a terminal disease barely a year after finding true love. The nightmare continued for the grieving widow, who was now successor trustee over their trust, and found herself suddenly caught in the fray of his children's emotions

---

[1] Forbes Best in State and Top Women in Wealth Awards were from 2022–2025. No compensation was given in return for the award.

when they wanted to spend their inheritance way too quickly. In the end, the change brought such strife that the responsibility passed to her deceased husband's best friend, yet not in time for the children to hold more grudges than love.

Yet tough situations don't have to be the end of the line. Or maybe it does. We have choices, even when trying to find common ground doesn't work. Changing a relationship, even when it doesn't improve, is a choice.

Your change can bring new people into your life, too. It can take you to new places, maybe even a new place in the (metaphorical) backyard you think you thoroughly know right now.

What happens if you let change do that for you?

What happens if you go beyond letting to embracing... or _____? You tell me.

6

Change Can Be the Loneliest Number

"The loneliest moment in someone's life is when they are watching their whole world fall apart, and all they can do is stare blankly."

F. Scott Fitzgerald

Death. Divorce. Retirement. They all come with major alterations in relationship and companionship—alterations that usher in loneliness—another characteristic of change.

Listen, it's okay to sit with loneliness for a while. Embrace The Suck, I say! There are lessons to be learned within that experience. As a matter of fact, I'd advise you not to run from it, as uncomfortable as it may be. When my marriage ended, I did a monumentally un-useful thing and ran headlong toward a new relationship, intent on finding that external validation I craved and "true love."

You can guess how well that went, right?

There's really no good reason to pretend you aren't afraid or lonely in the face of change, and all sorts of good reasons to sit with those feelings—for a little while. I'm not advocating that you build a home there. Maybe just pitch a tent for a while and make a sign post so you (and a therapist) can make your way back for occasional processing visits.

The CDC cites that social isolation and loneliness can increase a person's risk for heart disease, stroke, Type 2 diabetes, depression, anxiety, suicide, self-harm, dementia, and even an earlier death. A ton of research demonstrates significant links between social connection and mortality risk since the first landmark large-scale longitudinal epidemiological studies in 1979. That research found that people who lacked social connection were more than twice as likely to die than those with greater social connection despite similar age, health status, socioeconomic status, and health practices.[2]

The Surgeon General says a lack of social connection is as bad for your health as smoking, drinking, and inactivity. Yep.

Just realizing that change brings loneliness to us all is at least some form of solace. Jumping headfirst into anything is usually not the answer. Neither is staying put in the middle of it because it's not long-term healthy. What we are meant to do with that lonely feeling is to work through it. And that doesn't typically look the same for any of us.

---

[2] Berkman LF, Syme SL. *Social networks, host resistance, and mortality: a nine-year follow-up study of Alameda County residents.* Am J Epidemiol. 1979;109(2):186–204.

Much of this guide is to help you process some of these emotions and get you to the other side of them.

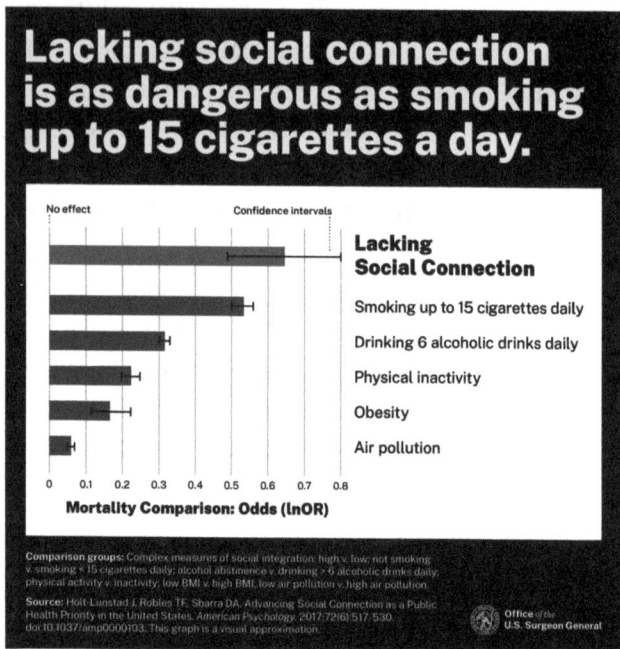

Lacking social connection is as dangerous as smoking up to 15 cigarettes a day.

Mortality Comparison: Odds (lnOR)

No effect — Confidence intervals

- Lacking Social Connection
- Smoking up to 15 cigarettes daily
- Drinking 6 alcoholic drinks daily
- Physical inactivity
- Obesity
- Air pollution

0   0.1   0.2   0.3   0.4   0.5   0.6   0.7   0.8

Comparison groups: Complex measures of social integration; high v. low; not smoking v. smoking < 15 cigarettes daily; alcohol abstinence v. drinking > 6 alcoholic drinks daily; physical activity v. inactivity; low BMI v. high BMI; low air pollution v. high air pollution.

Source: Holt-Lunstad J, Robles TF, Sbarra DA. Advancing Social Connection as a Public Health Priority in the United States. American Psychology. 2017;72(6):517-530. doi:10.1037/amp0000103. This graph is a visual approximation.

Office *of the* U.S. Surgeon General

For me, the antidote to loneliness ended up being action. *Not destructive action, friend.* Not a headlong rush toward external validation. I'm talking about—and I know you'll be shocked when I say it—making choices and acting on them. (Are you starting to detect a theme here?) From your place of loneliness, choose what you will *do* today that is productive. Will you finally shower? Get dressed? Do the grocery shopping? Go to church/synagogue/temple/bridge club/girls' night out? Organize the junk drawer? (No shame, we've all got them.) Research airfares and buy the plane ticket?

Stop staring blankly.

Settle on one activity *and do it.*

Force yourself to interact with people. Do things. Say YES.

Loneliness—like all the elements that change brings—has a positive aspect. A significant one is that it can be changed. There is no need to languish in isolation once you've mined it for the lessons it holds. All you need to do *once that work is done* is choose action.

7

Change Is Cyclical

To everything turn, turn, turn
There is a season turn, turn, turn
And a time to every purpose under Heaven

From *Turn! Turn! Turn!* by The Byrds

I've noticed that my identity undergoes a change about every five to seven years. Noticing this brought me incredible peace because now I know it's coming. I can brace for the process. Prepare for it, even! Oh, I do love a good plan.

My latest identity crisis arrived because that word "retirement' kept getting put in the same sentence as my name *in my own mind*. I'm not old enough to retire!

Narrator: Yes, she is.

Well, even if I am, I don't *want* to.

Narrator: Then don't.

The thing about change is that, sometimes, you get to define exactly what it is. Take retirement, for instance. Your definition might be, "Never touch a lick of the work

I've done for forty years ever again." And that's okay. My definition of retirement is not to stop working—I love what I do too much to set it aside. I'd be miserable, not advising people about their finances. I'd become the elderly lady in the corner office crooking a finger and saying, "Come here, sonny, let me tell you why venture capital isn't the way to go." And I'd be right, but I'd also be ignored and wouldn't that be a shame not just for me but also for sonny's portfolio?

So, the definition of retirement for me became a shift in how, when, and where I work rather than a cessation of work. I defined my retirement goals: be able to wake up late if I so choose, have time for exercise and tennis again, and be able to winter and work in a Florida community.

It took three years for me to work up the nerve to walk into this change. See? Even I, the Change Queen, can take a minute or two to embrace change.

In 2024, I bought my home in Naples, Florida. I now split my time between there and Huntsville, Alabama, with clients and offices in both locales—but a structure in place that reduced some of my workload instead of doubling it. It took hiring some great people and changing some roles so clients get the same high-quality service and delivery on commitments. This is how businesses grow and how clients get even better care if you structure it right. It's also how owners avoid burnout.

You can do this, too, if you want. Your choices through change can inch you into realizing certain things and/or learning different skills to help you live in your new situation. If change has walked you to an identity crossroads, plunked you down, and then decided to run off, it's okay. Feeling that you don't know who you are or what you want to become from here *is okay.* Your interests and passions might be nothing more than tumbleweeds rolling off in a stiff wind at this point, and *that's okay.* If staring in the mirror shows you not much more than a stranger, take a deep breath and know that *you're okay.*

Choose to set anxiety down (in whatever way works, including professional help if needed)—not that I have mastered this. Set aside, too, the inclination to define yourself by what you are not. Rather than say, "Well, I don't want to do that thing anymore," let's try to focus on what you'd like to do or be now, then take action that begins to put that into existence. You can choose to see this as a journey in self-discovery.

As with any journey, the process of embracing change won't be without its share of potholes, dead ends, and U-turns. And that's okay! Let those experiences serve as opportunities to dig deeper, take more steps, and make more choices. By doing so, you allow yourself to grow and become an even better version of yourself with each new change.

I've included some examples from my own life below that illustrate how change leads to wisdom. If you avoid change, then chances are higher that your personal growth will stagnate. And what kind of life is that? We're here to learn and grow. Change is life, remember?

This cyclical nature of change seems to add up to more and more wisdom and personal growth. It's as if you are supposed to accumulate nuggets of truth over time which equip you to contribute your learning back to the world around us. As you learn truths, you are forced to build skills ... at least, if you so choose.

1. Moving around so much as a kid, I was *never* in the "in crowd" and existed in a constantly uncomfortable state of trying to be liked and included (that doesn't change much). I learned, though, that instead of trying to please people to fit in, I could choose to just make everyone, no matter who they were, comfortable when they were with me. That meant I tried to understand whoever sat next to me in class or ran beside me at cross-country practice. Little did I know that I was skill-building for a future career.

2. As a youth who was constantly thrown into new places and faces, I learned—eventually—that in the throes of change, it's important to find one thing or two in life that you can control. For me, that meant I threw myself into studying. That gave me an excellent foundation of knowledge to step into a challenging career. And it gave me a workhorse attitude which wouldn't let go until the job was done well and thoroughly. This brought early success in my chosen career.

3. In my twenties and thirties, I found I was working fifty to sixty hours a week (and liking it). This produced a setup for multiple other changes which required building additional skills. I had to give up having a personal life (not hard since I loved who I worked with) but also had to figure out how to meet client needs and recruit and retain staff. It was retaining that was so hard. Every person in my

early days at Investor's Resource will tell you that I was a terrible boss and HR person! Well, except for Jill, who was my first licensed sales assistant and from whom I learned the value of investing in people around you. I paid her more than I'd ever paid anyone, and in return she opened my eyes to the value of letting her handle clients and certain needs instead of me. She was actually better at certain things, which was a sharp lesson for this hard-driving, goal-oriented, only child. It was too bad her husband moved her from Huntsville because I truly think she'd still be in my company today. Jill paved the way for others to grow and for my mindset to shift. I now know the value of investing in others. If they are successful, I will be successful.

4. The next phase of change came in my forties when it was evident I needed others who could carry out advisor-level duties. This forced a change and development of a new skill set for me: truly letting go—something beyond just delegation. I learned to stop telling people what to do (I know, hard to admit for an only child) and allowing them to carry out their role in maybe even better ways that I could have done or imagined. It was and is a gift to see them excel and bring complimentary skills to the table to uniquely handle client needs. But first, I had to lay down micro-management and dictatorship... in the nicest of ways.

5. At age fifty when the retirement question reared its head in my life, I found myself in a fat mess created by my own success. While happy, I couldn't seem to build a personal life. I had none except a few tennis teams. By 55 or so, I suffered burnout. I needed to change things because I'd spun up so many opportunities that structurally I had to make a huge shift in the company and give up some responsibility. This created a culture clash within the personalities and habits of the original team and the new hires. There was a lot of strife I didn't even know was going on, and it would take time to blend into the next phase of the company. Yet our folks pulled together, and the change allowed me to evolve again with renewed purpose and intent. It enabled me to slow down and think more, to develop a softer side, and to outwardly show the inner care I feel for people.

As you navigate the cycle of change as a self-discovery process, remember that it can be challenging. Allowing your identity to evolve and mature may be one of the most difficult challenges you'll face over a lifetime. Regardless, you'll have to face it one way or another, and you just may find that what you see on the other side is far greater than you could have imagined.

As we move through actions to take in the face of change in later chapters, hold to the truth that you have options. You can decide what you want to revive out your old identity and what you'd like to feature in the new one. Knitting together insights from what you are (or are not) doing or being—what behaviors you are exhibiting and what changes you need for fulfillment—is key to helping you move through change in your life and get the good of it.

There is no way to return to who you were before change blew in, but you can emerge wiser for the road ahead. You are fully capable of embracing the challenge of determining who you want to be and the course you wish to take. Maybe reading a few ways that change has brought wisdom into my life will help you think about how the changes in your own life could bring you wisdom, too.

8

Change Is the Story You Tell Yourself

Fortune [fawr-ch*uh*n]

noun

1. a large amount of money:

Those repairs will cost a fortune.

2. chance personified, commonly regarded as a mythical being distributing arbitrarily or capriciously the lots of life:

Perhaps Fortune will smile on our venture.

Over Labor Day weekend in 2022, my home in Huntsville caught fire. Based on that introduction, which definition of "fortune" do you think I'm going to focus on?

The water heater underneath the house blew up. This should have tripped a breaker. It didn't. It also should have terminated in the red clay, but I had a plastic radon barrier across the entire base of the house, and that plastic caught fire, spreading it across the whole crawl space of the house. That plastic *also* contained the fire within the crawl space, protecting the rest of the house from burning down.

So, instead of coming home to a pile of ashes, I came home to a huge smoke event. Yes, it was still a mighty mess to clean up, both literally and with the insurance claims. It was a change I didn't foresee and had to navigate immediately. I began by choosing to acknowledge the good fortune within the misfortune.

There is a debate about whether life happens to us or results from our actions. Is it random? Or is it that some people are just luckier than others? How much can we control?

Social scientists say luck is "the result of personal actions, an alchemy of openness to new experiences and a penchant for chance-taking" (Vild, 2022). If that is true, it is also true that you can make your luck by the way you welcome change. Ultimately, change is nothing if not a series of experiences we choose for ourselves. Either way, you get to play a role in managing the change experience.

The *Psychology Today* article "4 Ways to Improve Your Luck" explains it like this. "Those who view themselves as lucky tend to behave much differently than those who see their lives as plagued by bad breaks. Lucky people have this in common. They regularly change their routine, vary their environment, and mix with many people. This positive, go-getter attitude results in new experiences and the enthusiasm to take advantage of them" (Vild, 2022).

My home was uninhabitable during the cleanup and restoration process, which dragged on for nearly two *years*. Have you ever had an insurance claim that drags out for years? They do not like to keep mailing checks that long—at least, mine did not. They conveniently noticed I had a decorator doing work in the home at the same time that the restoration work was underway, which in their view had to be the reason the process needed so much time. As a result, they took away their payment of my monthly housing rental.

Did I mention they delivered this news to me on December 15, accompanied by a December 30 deadline?

With several more months of work needed before I could return to my home, I could easily have decided I'm just a person with bad luck. I began to reconcile myself to calling the owner of the home in which I'd been staying and switching the payments to come from my account because Lord knew I'd be unable to find something else within the two weeks that hold both Christmas and New Year's breaks. But, as with all change moments, I had a choice here. I could choose to believe that I am a person with *good* luck, not bad. This change could be an opportunity for joy, not a barrier. When viewing this new forced change through that lens, I thought, "You know what? My parents are taking their trip to Anna Maria Island on January 15. I'll just go down there with them. Furthermore, I'll see if the condo they got could simply extend its reservation, as it's the same cost to stay there for a month as it is to stay here in Huntsville, and there I can explore the island."

And then, once I got to Anna Maria Island, that train of new thought kept chugging down the tracks. That was my second trip to the island. I liked the tropical, warm, beach atmosphere. I'd been wanting to engage with the whole "do Florida" thing, so I decided I had a golden opportunity. If I had to spend extra money to house myself, I might as well do it at the beach!

I looked at homes in towns up and down the Gulf coast of Florida, ultimately purchasing one in Naples. With that, I took a huge step toward the next phase of my life—my version of retirement.

All of that enjoyment, growth, and forward movement happened because I decided that, rather than get mad and rail at the insurance company for forcing change, I'd think about their decision as a catalyst for good fortune in my life.

But what if you're not quite there yet? What if you've experienced a change that doesn't feel fortunate? You feel sad or overwhelmed, lost, or left behind instead. If that's where you are right now, it's okay to be there for a little while. I did, too, when my initial reaction was just to take on the costs of the house I'd been in when the change came. Consider, though, how your forced change might be of benefit to you. If you were to write the story of this change in your life, how would you give it a happy ending? There's your good fortune.

This brings us to a crucial point we must acknowledge. You truly are a person of "good fortune" first because you have time to think about it. Right now, there is someone else who is experiencing a change that time cannot heal. There is someone with little time left or who won't get to live beyond their loss or change. If time can heal your situation, then this in itself is fortunate.

Continue your good fortune by choosing to override your feelings and emotions that frame the situation as bad luck. Create additional good fortune for yourself right now through a succession of attitudes and decisions. As long as you are breathing, you can choose not to allow a singular point of loss to be the defining event for the rest of your life.

Finding the golden nuggets, no matter the situation, is complicated when facing change alone. If you don't reach out to the people around you, you'll increase the chances of change suffocating and leaving you hopeless. Moving back toward your friends or spheres of influence sometimes takes significant effort, yet doing so or daring to meet others in your community, city, or even worldwide can help you better handle and maximize your change. Think about it like Newton's Third Law: each action has an equal and opposite reaction. What you put out comes directly back to you.

So how does that work, especially in the middle of change, and how can you find more fortune in your circumstances? Part of your answer is likely part of the golden nugget you are meant to find. There is purpose in it all.

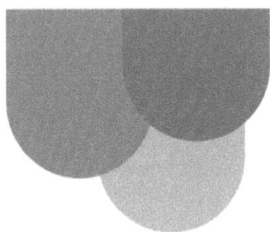

ACTIONS IN THE FACE OF CHANGE

9

Moving On vs. Moving Forward

"Do the best you can until you know better. Then when you know better, do better."

Maya Angelou

B efore I begin the section on actions you can take in the face of change, it's important to ensure we're speaking the same language. Namely, I need you to understand the differences in my mind between "moving on" and "moving forward."

When people say, "Move on," I hear, "Forget it, leave it behind, just move on."

Where's the learning in that? The growth? It doesn't exist. Moving on means you're living the definition of insanity, which is to keep doing the same thing while expecting different results. It's like cashing out your investment account in a stock market correction *after* it's lost twenty percent. You probably were coached that risk was part of the deal, but when you experienced it to a certain pain point, you caved in and sold. This means you not only lost the twenty percent, you also lost what you could have gained. You then move on. Let it go. And then, a few years later, the market corrects again. And, again, you cash in and lose even more.

Moving *forward* through change does not mean forgetting the change that happened and just walking on anyway. We are all the sum of our good and bad experiences. In order to move forward as you navigate change, you'll carry with you the previous experiences in the form of lessons learned, references, and reminders. No rule says that to grow into a better self and create newer, better choices, you must forget your old self. It's quite the opposite.

When you try to erase your past and just move *on*, you leave behind the version of yourself that helped you to face the change or fear that developed during that time. But to move *forward*, you must remember some of the skills you attained while combating unfavorable circumstances. Does it suit a tennis player to enter match after match without learning from the previous ones? Of course not. Serena Williams doesn't lose a match and think, "Oh well, move on." She and millions of other elite athletes watch tape, carefully scrutinizing what happened for any lessons it might divulge. They then move forward, assimilating those lessons into who they are as they step into the next competition.

Each of your past occurrences helped you get to your present moment. They also equipped you to shape what comes next.

When you choose to move forward with the experienced survivor self that has learned from each stage of your life, you can significantly contribute to your future. Rather than walking blindly on, you're traveling armed with reminders of how far you've come. Recognition of that growth gives you a needed boost or push to keep going or step in another direction. It warms you and comforts you. It can bring joy. It can even validate why you've done what you've done—left behind some things and retained others. This happens while you continue to search and add to your life through self-reflection.

"I am entirely too old and too tired to start mining my past for lessons and moving forward," you might say.

Are you breathing?

Then you're not too old.

Take a nap if you're too tired. (Rest is not a reward, it's a requirement.)

Maybe your inclination to bury the experience deep, never to be unearthed again, is the exact right response for today. Or perhaps you might think: *This sounds like counseling crap, and I'm just not that person.*

Narrator: Of course, you know she doesn't agree and that perhaps what you are doing today to get through the day may not be exactly long term optimal.

No one said it's easy.

Should you choose to take this challenge to move forward, it in part means that you'll need to grant yourself some additional think-time. It's not woo-woo, and you don't have to go to some made-over '70s Woodstock retreat to do it. It doesn't have to fit any particular mold. I would suggest that if you don't do it, then you partially rob yourself of the ability to speed up the processing-process. We all want to get to a point of actually deriving some benefit from our pain or discomfort.

This type of self-reflection can start at any point of your life and executing it can take many forms. Maybe it's an exercise of meditation or journaling or prayer. Something else? Pick your poison. Whatever form you choose to try, the process tends to go faster when you have a track to run on. This is especially true since not everyone relishes the idea of setting aside time for something they don't have to do. Knowing that, I suggest some questions people ask themselves as they begin the task of self-reflection:

- What are some significant milestones that I've accomplished?
- What places and/or situations would I like to avoid entering again?
- What have I learned in each stage when I divide my life into periods by years, age, or circumstances?
- What does this latest learning do for me, given my current circumstance, outlook, and future?
- What have been my priorities?
- What are my priorities now?
- Where does or has my spiritual life fit into each life change?
- What limitations lie ahead, and how am I (now) equipped to deal with them?

If you'd like a reflection system that doesn't require too much time each month but offers a big return, I'd recommend taking a look at Susannah Conway's *Unravel Your Year*. She graciously provides this annual journal for free each year on her website. It provides an opportunity to do a deep-dive at the end of the year, then prep for the year ahead. There are monthly check-in pages to fill in, which allows you to easily review the year's highlights of experience, growth, and learning at the journal's end.

A while back, I advised a woman who was the only single sister out of four with no children of her own. She was grappling with the change of losing her father and being a large part of his caregiving team in his later years. She'd built a successful career, so when her father passed away and left his wealth behind, she had no daily need for the funds. In the face of the change his death brought, though, she took some time for self-reflection. Did she want to keep going down the course she'd charted long ago? His death woke her up to her own mortality, which led her to thoughts of legacy. Her sisters all had children and thus looked upon a large part of their legacy differently, she said. In her mind, she had the choice to keep on going in life and sort of try and move on from her dad's death. Before his passing, she'd planned a quiet retirement life. She foresaw no changes to that plan.

Until, with his death, she did.

She made a choice. She asked herself, "Would the world be better for my having walked upon it?" She'd never asked herself that question in that sort of way until her father died. It birthed a whole new perspective on living.

She decided a change was in order, and together, we began to work out what that could look like for her. She shared her values and beliefs in what could make things better, then we ordered her resources to be in alignment with the realization of those goals.

If, when her dad died, she had simply made herself

move on—forget it and keep going—both she and this world would be a slightly dimmer place. Because she took the time to mine the change for lessons, because she saw it as an opportunity for choice, we all live in a slightly better world today.

A rich life cannot come if all you want to do is forget.

When you choose to move forward with a self that has learned from each change of your life and remembers the new wisdom, it can significantly contribute to your future and others'. It can remind you how far you've come or give you a needed boost to keep going or step in another direction. It can validate why you left behind some things and retained others. In the end, what you learn can warm you and comfort you, bringing you joy and the strength to keep moving forward.

Just remember to let your past teach you. There are many lessons in loss and change back there. It is not often spotless but marked by the passage of time and life. It is filled with examples of how you have been able to endure, adapt, and find golden nuggets of wisdom. The past can be your driving force to a future more incredible than you imagined. It can ignite a fire only to be extinguished upon reaching your destination. It can be a catalyst for your growth and resilience.

Now, let's look at some specific actions you can take in the face of change.

10

Chat with Change

"If you're going through hell, keep going."

Source: Unknown

I've heard the above quote several times in my life and yet didn't realize until I sat down to write that we are unsure who originally said it. There exist so many famous people who said it at one time or another that we just don't know where it began.

I think that's indicative of our need to rush when things get tough, and I'm going to encourage you as your first action step in the face of change... to take no action.

Yes, I mean it.

Some decisions are really best made early rather than late, and you can make those decisions when you are still reeling and in the middle of change. There is a wisdom in knowing when to set aside decent advice and when to take on things that move the needle—whether you change or whether you don't.

Unless it would cause ongoing harm, I ask you to stop

and stay in the experience for a little while. Be in it. Look around in this space and let yourself feel, consider, and know what this is like—to face and be in this change.

Do you know an avid gardener? My mother is the green thumb in my family; I think I have a black thumb—give me a plant and it has a 50/50 chance of living. When I garden, usually it's getting weeds out of the flowerbeds or small but necessary things that most yard services don't do. I do it as fast as possible. I hate pulling weeds, and yet I hate seeing them more. There is a small amount of satisfaction I get from knowing that I'm killing an insidious cancer in my yard when I do it, yet I still rush through it. Quite the opposite is true for my mom. She will weed a flowerbed or dig crabgrass out of a lawn and she actually *enjoys* it. She immerses herself in the experience. She is "one" with the garden. She is making that corner of the world a better place while loving the experience of being outside in the beauty of nature.

While I do not share my mother's level of patience in the garden, I do believe that taking your time when handling emotions and managing change is important. There is deep value in being patient in that experience.

Maybe one day that belief will translate over to my yard work.

Narrator: It will not.

Avoid the inclination to rush through whatever hell has come into your life because, in that rush, you can miss some valuable learning that's needed for the road ahead. Also, not giving yourself time to process through this can result in mental and emotional overload that comes back to haunt you whenever you *do* take a moment to breathe.

As crazy as it sounds in our hurried world of today, there are distinct benefits to taking your time.

First, you minimize mistakes and risks. Inevitably, the more time you give yourself to examine the details, consider various angles, conduct research, or ask questions, the better odds you'll have of making decisions that stick and make you happy. Plenty of great decisions can be made in this time of chatting with change. There's no rush to make many of them. Side note: I hate the well-intentioned advice to "wait a year" when well-intentioned friends and family tell newly widowed spouses things like, "Don't sell the house or make major financial changes immediately." Who came up with that? This is a perfect situation for a mental chat with yourself (and probably an advisor). It's a prompt to engage in a conversation within yourself and others while you go about living. It's the very opposite of sitting, avoiding, and stagnating. That can really limit options, so when I say there's no rush, I do so with the expectation that financially you are looking all angles. When you do that, "wait a year" can be in direct opposition to prudent financial strategy for your particular situation.

Second, taking your time protects your overall well-being. Rushing about stresses your nervous and immune systems. It accelerates your heart rate and can increase the release of stress hormones throughout your body. If you are led to make life-altering decisions after a change, then realize that will come with stress. Why compound your strain by rushing into what's next—unless, of course, there's a reason?

Narrator: This is where she points out the value of having a great financial advisor instead of one who's just checking boxes.

It's a balance. When you chat with change, and you're really honest with yourself, you allow your own instincts to join with sound advice from others, enabling you to determine how long is best to wait to tackle things and what decisions are best to just plow through and make. There just are no blanket answers.

Third, taking your time creates space for acceptance. It's common to want to speed through things that hurt or make you uncomfortable. Even when the discomfort stems from something you asked for, it's still not a pleasant experience. It's no wonder that there is not a desire to linger in it. But don't move so quickly.

Find your version of gardening. Be present in the acts of tilling, planting, weeding, and watering.

Breathe and realize that lingering is needed sometimes. It can help you understand your experiences and feelings and set a proper plan for moving forward. Lingering helps you take each day as it comes and make sense of your emotions in a way that allows you to move forward healthily and productively. As you till the soil and chat with change, here are some guidelines for your thoughts:

Give thanks. Gratitude is an attitude. This statement may sound cheesy, but it's a simple way to think about how you navigate the world. Loss and subsequent change can stump anyone at any given moment. Those things may leave us wondering, "Why me?" And though it's a valid question, an equally valid one is, "How can I practice gratitude despite what is happening to me right now?" Practicing gratitude does not dissolve your right to feel pain, express your fears and sorrows, cry in agony, or shout out in anger. You can still do those because humans are meant to experience and express various emotions. You can add to that an expression of gratitude. It is yet another emotion to add to your arsenal, and it helps you see the good of what you have instead of focusing on what you don't.

Be open. You're probably familiar with the term "know-it-all." In case you aren't, the phrase describes a person who has an answer to every question and knows something about everything. One danger in showcasing their knowledge is limiting additional learning and perspective from anyone or anything else. It can offend people and be an isolator. Be open to new people, new experiences, new ideas, and new lines of thinking, which can bring you more in tune with each situation's silver lining.

Say "Yes." When you are facing change, the last thing you probably want to do is introduce more change. But sometimes you should. Keep in mind that change is not an inherently "bad thing." It just sometimes gets a bad reputation. Change can be really good, especially regarding the suggestions of people we know, like, and trust. It can also be good to say "yes" when interacting with people you'd like to emulate or know better. Allow people with your best interests to introduce you to things outside your comfort zone. Say "yes" to their invitations and introductions. Say "yes" to their suggestions, offerings, and connections. They may lead you to people and places you'd have never chosen that may become precious experiences for your next chapter.

Drop the dead weight. This one can be especially difficult. When you want to dig deep and create a new future, you may need to leave people, places, and things behind. Those who question your motivations or are unwilling to support you through your new endeavors may or may not play a role in your tomorrow. Only you can decide that. And while they may not necessarily understand your choices today, it's crucial that they not interfere with the process. Likewise, the environment in which you find yourself can become a hindrance. Evaluate where that truth lies, what should stay, and what should go. It is rarely easy to let go of the things you love or have become attached to, even when they no longer serve you. Maybe dropping the dead weight means keeping the people and places but re-framing how much interaction you have or to what emotional level you'll go. You can give yourself some grace here and make the necessary adjustments at a palatable pace. Conversely, you must hold yourself accountable for what needs to go and eventually get where you can. Your "fortune" and your quality of life depend on it.

Allow yourself to receive the fortune of choosing to see and explore the possibilities, the people, and the opportunities at your fingertips. You are here for a reason. The blessings await!

There is fertile ground right where you're standing (or sitting, or lying, if the change has leveled you). Breathe in. Breathe out. Be in it for the time you need to find its lessons and a way forward that works. I bet there are lessons or new understandings you could think of right now that resulted from a change you have experienced. That's exactly how it's supposed to work.

11

Better or Bitter?

Bitter [bit-er]

adjective

characterized by intense antagonism or hostility:

bitter hatred

Better [bet-er]

adjective

of superior quality or excellence, of superior suitability, advisability, desirability, acceptableness, etc.; preferable:

better suited for action

I found an article in *Psychology Today* that listed nine habits that can make you bitter. Among them were believing things will never get better and thinking you have less control over your life than you do. These are particularly interesting regarding the concept of facing and addressing change. The habits, or attitudes as I call them, can be the barrier between being swallowed up by the emotions that come with change or allowing those emotions to help blossom you into your next phase of life.

Feelings of anger, hurt, and resentment characterize bitterness. Bitter people feel they have suffered too many bad experiences or been regularly subjected to unfair treatment. As a result, they become pessimistic, hardened, disheartened, and sometimes downright mean.

Change presents a major opportunity to choose: better or bitter?

You can see an injustice that *destroys* you or an injustice that *ignites* you.

A lack of comfort that leaves you cold or teaches you to stitch a blanket.

Abandonment as desolation or an opportunity for new relationships.

Hey, it's a choice! Just like you can choose to see opportunities, you can also choose to see lack of opportunities.

Here's the kicker: Whichever you choose, you're right.

Even in situations where you think you have no control (i.e. divorce, health, caregiving), you do still have choice. Just because you feel a lack of control doesn't mean you are stuck. It's the feeling stuck that can really breed bitterness.

For instance, when settling assets during a divorce, there is sometimes a push to put the house, sometimes quite a large asset, in the female's name (assuming she also gets primary custody of the kids, so they experience the least change possible). So she loses other assets, which ultimately affects her income and standard of living. That, in turn, can be the beginning of resentment as she may come to devalue that house.

This isn't just a shameless plug to suggest having a

trained advisor by your side who can make recommendations as to fair and equitable division of assets, it's also a means to help you plan for things that seem to be less in your control and brainstorm choices around that!

I urge you to allow change, even the foulest, to open you to something better. Think of it like this. While some changes are much more challenging to navigate, there is a place where you can find a bright spot, a glimmer of hope, that leads you to your next stage positively and beneficially. Train yourself to seek out and see the bright spots. If you are a caregiver, train yourself to take time for yourself and talk to a buddy about all you are personally going through... as hard as that might be. Give yourself permission to leave your loved one and give yourself the mental reset time. You'll be a better you—for you. And in turn, you'll be a better you—for them.

"Fine, I'll stop throwing plates at the wall or sobbing mercilessly into my pillow or throwing myself into this situation and not giving my own needs attention. How do I get to being better... and be sure I don't one day spill over to bitter?"

I have a plan—and some exercises—for that. (I can imagine your surprise.)

Step 1—Pinpoint Your Anger or Anxiety. First, permit yourself to be angry. Permit yourself to realize your discomfort. Let yourself steep in it until your fingers get pruny. This should take, oh, maybe a day. If you thought you buried it, dig it up and dance with it because it was never going to stay buried for the long term anyway. Anger doesn't do that. It is an emotion that demands its due process. So have at it. Be mad. Be furious. Go ahead and give energy to your anger. It's just another emotion of your complex self. Go ahead and say it out loud. You're mad! Identify exactly what you're angry about. Get to the root of it. It isn't that he cheated; it's that he lied *and* he cheated. It isn't that you were fired; it's that being fired made you feel discarded. If you're going to do this, go all the way. Dive into that anger until you're right there at its start.

Step 2—Call It Out. Now that you know the root of why you're mad (you're embarrassed, ashamed, disappointed, disillusioned, disenfranchised, righteously indignant, etc.), say it out loud. "I am absolutely furious because _____." Out loud. Listen to the ring of your own voice in the air, naming what has angered you, dragging it out of the shadows, disinfecting it with sunlight.

Step 3—Release Your Resentment. With the source of your anger now present in the air, blow it away. Literally. I'm telling you to blow away the echo of the words you just said. Release them. They hold no more power over you because this is what you *choose*. Send them on their way, banishing their energy from yours. You do not choose to be someone cloaked in a resentment that subconsciously repels good people, opportunities, and circumstances from your life. You're way too smart for that at this point in this book. Is this release and banishment of resentment easy? It's as hard as you make it. Remember, whatever you choose, that's what you choose.

I know that finding the bright spot is often easier said than done. Much of it comes down to whether you're innately optimistic or pessimistic, and the stats show that we're pretty evenly split on that. So—I've got fifty-percent odds that a pessimist is reading this book. To you I say this— optimism is a learned thinking style. Would you look at that? Even in your pessimism, you have a choice. You can choose to think as an optimist—or, at minimum, find a more real or practical version of your pessimism!

As an optimist, you generally have an easier time finding the silver lining. If you are a person who usually sees the glass half empty, it may be more difficult. Either way, there are two primary methods to walk into betterness instead of bitterness.

1. Adjust your mindset.
2. Take action.

Do not mix up the order of those steps!

Mindset is a set of beliefs or perceptions people hold about themselves, who they are, and what's available to them. Your mindset about situations can either help or hinder you when change comes. It's crucial to cultivate a growth mindset.

Stanford professor Dr. Carol Dweck defines a growth mindset as a belief that achieving success depends on each person's time, effort, and persistence. A growth mindset affords you the capacity to look for the bright spot. Even in the most dire situations, you can train yourself to sit back, examine your circumstances, and be convinced that you can move forward positively. Even negative self-talk or comments from naysayers can be overcome and incorporated as a part of your progress.

Taking action feels like progress because it is exactly that. There is little time to focus on the negative or wallow in your circumstances when you're in motion-making progress. While it's true that change sometimes calls for a moment of inaction, you don't get to stay there for good. Otherwise, you won't make it to the other side. When it's time to get back into the groove of things, small actions can lead to big rewards. Small actions and big rewards equal no time to let bitterness manifest. In turn, you become victorious over your circumstances; you become better.

Now, this will look different for different people. Simply getting out of bed every day might be the action that reflects the hope you've adopted. For others, seizing a new opportunity or reclaiming a forgotten goal or vision could reflect the internal mindset shift. The specific action itself doesn't matter. That's all relative and personal. Regardless of your particular change, what matters most is that you don't become imprisoned in inaction because you allowed yourself to become mired in bitterness. You deserve more than that, as does the life that awaits you.

12

Let It Go

"You cannot win your future if you cannot forgive your past."
Ikechukwu Joseph

L et me tell you about a dear woman I had the honor of serving during a major change in her life. Her husband battled a debilitating disease that inevitably led him to a hospital bed. A month rolled off the calendar. By that time, he was long past thriving—just surviving, breath to breath, with the constant aid of medical technology.

Knowing him, knowing his heart and mind and wishes, she made the excruciating decision to withdraw aid. And even though she knew that's what he wanted and even though she loved him enough to do what he wanted, she still struggled in the aftermath to forgive herself. Her nature was to nurture life, not usher it out of this phase and into the next.

We had discussed their situation for years and knew what changes would occur if he were to pass away first. Before we could really even get to this, based on experience with others, I counseled her as I'll advise you here: forgive yourself and go into the discussions for potential financial restructuring with a clear, uncluttered mind. Many times when one spouse dies, there is a drop in income—pensions, social security, etc. That calls for the repositioning of other assets, and you should make those decisions quickly but without feelings which cause doubt. Having an advisor to share the pain and provide the logical, impartial planning is crucial.

If you're in a place of unforgiveness toward yourself, tell yourself your story but put somebody else in your role. Would you forgive that person? I'm guessing yes. How long, and for what reason, have you withheld forgiveness from yourself? A week? A year? Multiple years?

At its core, forgiveness is making conscious choices to let go of resentment, anger, disappointment, or embarrassment. That doesn't mean you can forget whatever caused the feelings. But it can mean that they no longer hold you in their grasp.

That's because forgiveness itself is a state of change. It operates along a spectrum. And just like any other change, it takes time and practice. Although it'd be nice to forgive yourself and automatically wake up the next day without any lingering negativity—and that sometimes happens— you might find yourself in need of renewing internal forgiveness with each new day for a while.

It's a valid question to ask, "Am I withholding grace from myself?" or, "Has any self-inflicted agony or pain become so normal that I barely think about it anymore?" If the answer to either question is in the affirmative, then some form of bondage is happening. Your burden, whether you consciously realize it or not, weighs on your mind, body, and spirit. It's easy to slip into not letting a decision or action go. Yet, there are consequences for this.

According to the Mayo Clinic, not forgiving yourself results in:

- Bringing anger and bitterness into new relationships and experiences
- Becoming so wrapped up in the wrong that you can't enjoy the present
- Becoming depressed, irritable, or anxious
- Feeling at odds with your spiritual beliefs
- Losing valuable and enriching connections with others

To be human is to have flaws, do stupid things, and make mistakes. Hopefully, you do this less as time passes. The idea is that your strengths outweigh your weaknesses and that your good choices outweigh your bad ones over time. If you don't let go of what didn't go well, feelings like anger, bitterness, depression, irritability, and anxiety creep in. This has a huge negative impact on your overall well-being. Too often, you change your outlook on life and the world for the worse. It becomes difficult to see the possibilities of what *can be* because of what *has been*. It then consumes you.

In order to quiet your subconscious, you might need a little outside help to realize that mistakes are just part of life and that forgiveness is indeed possible. Counseling can prove exceptionally valuable. It is one of the best investments I've ever made. One very wise psychologist told me that, for some people, experiencing depression is like trying to swim with a rock tied to their ankles. Even if you aren't ordinarily receptive to it, counseling and even medication may help you drop the extra weight and begin making progress.

Forgiving yourself brings a fresher, newer perspective to living. You can then move forward into a healthier, more evolved, state of being with higher self-esteem. Cut the rope. Release the rock. Swim freely in the abundant waters of life. Forgive yourself for whatever you did in the face of that change.

13

Count It Up

"Every accomplishment starts with the decision to try."

John F. Kennedy

C ongratulations! You've earned yourself a short chapter with a possibly long exercise. It's one I hope you will do and refer back to over time, especially if you find yourself in need of a mental boost.

The average life expectancy for a woman in the United States is eighty years, according to the Centers for Disease Control.

Eighty years.

Have you ever stopped to consider what your years until now have included?

Have you learned how to love and be loved? Made peace with whatever difficulties your childhood brought? Purchased property? Figured out how to get a credit card? (Figured out how to *pay off* a credit card?) Learned which foods do what for your health and well-being? Grown human beings within your body? Raised human beings into adulthood? Been a survivor of a big health event? Traveled somewhere other than your hometown? Earned a degree—or more? Traded your work for money that you then used to obtain nourishment in the forms of food, shelter, clothing, and experiences? Survived surgeries or sicknesses? Bought a vehicle? Learned to play an instrument? Lost weight and kept it off?

You've accomplished so much up until this point—but have you stopped to count it up?

This is the chapter where you do just that.

"Wait, wait, wait," you say. "I'm busy, with a million things remaining on my to-do list, and I'm not about being boastful anyway."

First of all, boasting requires *excessive* pride. If you haven't spent time thinking about your accomplishments in a long while (or ever), then you're so far from *excessive* that boasting is in another hemisphere.

Second, if you truly want to be effective in accomplishing whatever remains, then your brain needs to be rewarded for everything it's done thus far. Your job is to trip the lever that releases the dopamine to make your brain happy. Guess what trips the lever?

Yes. Taking a little while to revel in your accomplishments thus far. You (and your brain) then enjoy the good feeling of satisfaction with life thus far, and you're primed to keep going so that satisfaction continues.

Now that you're on board with the idea, let's get started acknowledging your accomplishments! You could think of these in whatever time period makes the most sense for you. Maybe, as I did above, you look at your life to date. Or perhaps you'd like to consider one goal you have and then list the steps you've already completed toward achieving that goal. Whichever of those options just resonated most strongly, go with it.

Get a pen. Go ahead, I'll wait.

Ready?

Now, either in the blank spaces within these pages or your journal or paper, write. Start with the first thing that comes to mind as an accomplishment. Pause. Read what you've written. Revel in it. You did that.

You.

Did.

That.

Now write down something else you've done.

And another.

And another.

Keep going.

Do it according to top accomplishments in a decade. Do it according to milestones with money, career, or finances. Do it with challenges you've overcome mentally.

Or celebrate the best thing you did today. What was it? What's the best thing you did all month? All year?

Spend as much time with this as it takes to get your brain oriented toward what you've already done instead of what you still want/need to do. Take an hour. Take a month! Enjoy that dopamine.

At some point, you'll begin to feel a sense of completion with this task. That will come before you have listed everything you've ever accomplished in your life, but after you've experienced a deep-seated sense of satisfaction with yourself. After this happens—and only *after* it happens—write down a goal you currently have. It can be long-term or short, personal or professional.

Now write down at least the first step you'll need to take in order to achieve that goal. If you do not know the first step, then the thing you write down is, "Figure out the first step to achieving this." When you have finished this step, pause.

Acknowledge that you have completed that first step.

Enjoy your dopamine.

And keep going.

14

Use What You Know

"Knowledge is knowing a tomato is a fruit. Wisdom is knowing not to put it in a fruit salad."

Miles Kingston

D ivorce is one of those tough life situations that half of married Americans experience at least once. You make a vow, "for better or for worse," to plow through life together no matter what. The problem arises when life brings a need for change that doesn't coincide with the commitment of "until death do us part."

I'm a big believer in commitments. I also have learned that this requires making fewer of them so that I am able to truly honor them and do what I say I will do. I have not shared much with many about my two marriages. Both times, I married the man who was my best friend. Both times, we were exceptionally transparent with one another about all the feelings and changes between us. The difference with my second divorce was that, by then, I had learned from the mistakes of my first marriage.

Unfortunately, there was more to learn, and my second marriage didn't survive either.

We, then I, went to counseling every week for over a year until I made the choice to end it. I spent many hours at home in the spare bedroom crying, painting, praying, and trying to figure out why I wasn't happy with a wonderful man—and meanwhile being who I needed to be for the clients and coworkers to whom I'd made a commitment. No one knew about the state of our marriage except the two of us, our families, a few close friends, and the counselor.

It was awful. I didn't want to get another divorce and hurt the person I cared most about in the world. In the end, I realized that I had to run *toward change*.

The truth I came to was that my husband deserved more than I could give, and he wasn't able to change in ways I needed. After much work, something didn't resonate or change for either of us. I still really hate that. And still, one day, a switch flipped, and suddenly, I ran toward the change that challenged the interpretation of every value I'd ever had around love and marriage.

When I counsel people on the divorce topic, often I encounter them at the point of frustration or anger while they are trying to divide assets. This can get messy financially if you don't know what you are doing—or if only one party knows what they are doing and attempts to take advantage of the other. When you make the decision to accept that you are going in a certain direction—or you have no choice—then is the time to gather your wits, put on your Big Girl Panties, and get some help to navigate the road. No sense in walking alone.

You, too, possess the ability to override the basic human instinct of flight away from change. You can choose to run straight toward it and even fight through it, especially if you take on some mental training exercises.

One such exercise is to focus on what's known rather than developing an obsession with what's not. This makes marching into the unknown more palatable. Nathan Furr and Susannah Harmon Furr (2022), authors of the *Harvard Business Review* article "How to Overcome Your Fear of the Unknown," explain that "uncertainty and possibility are two sides of the same coin." That implies your relationship with and response to change both lay in your perspective. You can choose to see change as something negatively life-altering or as a door opening to new opportunities.

In order to re-frame your perspective of change, focus on what you are sure of rather than being consumed with what you don't know.

Make Lists. List-making helps you get things out of your head and onto paper. It relieves the stress of mentally carrying out what is bothering you. It also helps to see something written so that you can reconcile its place in your life. An alternative to "pros and cons" is to answer a few questions:

- What do I now know about this change that would affect my future?
- What did I fear the most before this change?
- What "golden nugget" did I receive?
- What was the most significant thing I learned that applied to my next chapter of life?

- How has this change moved me toward (or away from) my top goal?
- What things beyond my present situation would I like to happen in my lifetime because of this change?

Take Action. Nothing beats the fear of the unknown like action. Taking action allows you to be productive and to learn. Not only do you learn with each step, but you also gain momentum. That momentum can make the difference between leaning into your change and letting it consume you. These actions don't have to be gigantic leaps into the unknown. Instead, they can be baby steps that slowly get you closer and closer to where you need to be.

Ask Hard Questions: Change has an uncanny way of making us all doubt what we believe. The deeper the change, the harder and more pervasive are the questions. Surround yourself with people who can help you make it hour to hour, day to day, and know that tomorrow is a new day. And know that it's okay to question your values and the things in which you believe. If your experience is anything like mine, even if our beliefs were completely different, I would trust that learning to be invaluable.

15

Choose Caution, Not Fear

"The oldest and strongest emotion of mankind is fear, and the oldest and strongest kind of fear is fear of the unknown."

H.P. Lovecraft

The situation: It was 2003, and I was so tired. I'd been through hell. Every morning, I dragged myself into the office at 7:30 a.m. and worked late into the evening talking with clients. The dot-com bubble had burst, and nothing I did seemed to work—not for me, and not for the clients. Because our compensation was tied to performance, and all accounts across all markets were sinking, payroll shrank as tensions rose. Every day was pretty much the same. Digest the losses, attempt to minimize them without doing everything that history teaches we shouldn't, and communicate our thoughts and actions to clients from sunup to sundown. Rinse and repeat the next day. And the next. Crash like crazy on the weekends because that's all I had in me. Get up and do it all over. While I can boast now that clients seemed to fare better than those of our competitors (no, my compliance department would never allow me to say that), I was really proud of our results in an unprecedented market. Yet I've never been so physically exhausted.

What happened: In the 1990s, I'm not even sure "caution" was in the vocabulary of most investors. But as we rolled closer to a new millennium, fear arose around Y2K. Warnings abounded that every computer would shut down at 12:01 a.m. as the year turned over to 2000, and the world would stop.

Given that you're sitting here reading this book decades later, it's clear the world did not stop.

It did, however, enter into an adjustment period unlike any before. Though Y2K fears evaporated in January 2000 and we all breathed in the sweet taste of relief, it didn't last.

Caution set in that year as broad markets like the S&P 500 lost 9%. But what happened in the tech stocks was far different and far worse. Those were averaging double or triple the losses of blue-chip companies. No one had seen anything like it before, and the fear mounted since many investors had loaded up on the investments during the 1990s.

From its peak on March 10, 2000, the tech-dominated NASDAQ Composite plunged 78% over the next twenty months—from 5,048 to 1,114. It seesawed through 2003 and landed at only 2,009.

I remember every day of these horrible 1,132 days of markets falling.

Time Magazine named it: The Decade from Hell. (Cover Story: December 9, 2009)

Even today, the dot-com bust makes any other stock

market correction look like a hiccup. It blindsided financial advisors and economic forecasters alike.

Sure, there'd been a crash in 1987. The market fell 22.6% but regained over half within a mere two days of trading sessions. By 1989, the market had fully recovered. In contrast, this crash had no end in sight. As each day passed, a little more fear crept into the hearts and minds of us financial advisors. It was a chilling time for us that washed many out of the business.

It sucked the air right out of most of us and developed an amazing skill for those who survived: being comfortable operating in the complete unknown. We survivors say we stayed in because we have a screw loose. We learned to mentally operate with some sense of clearheaded-ness, no matter the degree of change afoot.

We are all instilled with a sense of caution. It alerts us to danger. It warns us to be careful. This sense does not discriminate based on gender, class, or socio-economic status. If you've been on this planet longer than a millisecond, you've experienced that caution—which is not the same thing as fear. It's the keys between your fingers as you walk alone through an unlit parking lot. It's the *knowing* that sets the hairs on the back of your neck up and turns your feet in the other direction. That's caution that we sometimes mistake for fear.

I've been asked more than once, "How do you work in a world where everything is so uncertain?" and never more so than when the discussion turns to the dot-com crash. My initial answer is that the investment world—to a large extent—is very certain. After a few decades of working in it, you start to figure that out. One of the tenets of how I, and now *we*, have done things at the office is that certain "caution flags" go up when markets correct at certain levels. When they violate a threshold to the downside, I don't feel fear, but I do note the "violation." It usually means that newer or perhaps more conservative clients tend to call in with concerns. But I would add that this happens less and less often each year—which I hope means we are educating our clients well.

If the market continues down to my next threshold level, that's another caution flag. At the third caution flag, there's an even chance the market recovers or continues dropping so that's another decision point for us. This is where I feel some nervous anticipation—not that the sky will fall, but that we may have to take action on certain client portfolios.

I only really incorporated some of this formally into our investment process after living through the dot-com bust. That experience is singular in its existence—not only in terms of market volatility but also the rampant fear because of mass ignorance. My point in rehashing some of this is not to brag on what we did but to focus on what a teachable experience the whole time was... once I could get past the hell.

Those lessons and the skills that support them helped me survive the fear when the next big challenge came, the Great Recession of 2008. I learned firsthand that the concepts of caution and fear are different. A healthy dose of caution teaches you to be wise and honor your intuition. My lesson: Recognize patterns and put in place the systems to manage them. It's a business lesson, though for you it may be a personal one.

In the process of trying to navigate, caution can be unhealthy if it cripples you into a state of fear. That fear then keeps you from moving forward or taking leaps. It causes you anxiety and stress. It is a fear generally rooted in the unknown. The unknown makes humans uncomfortable because we can't predict it, which leaves us feeling powerless to affect the outcome.

And if you can't affect the outcome, then you might be forced to face a harmful one, right?

But what's the alternative? To sit at home on your couch, never going outside? Never even using your phone to reach out beyond the safe walls you've constructed?

Come on. You were meant for far more than your own isolation. That's *why* you have the innate sense of caution. It's there to give you a warning *as you move out into the world.*

So, rather than avoid the chance to live your life, how about you embrace your internal caution? You have the power to decide right now to work with it instead of living in dread of that moment. You can equip yourself to move forward armed with senses tuned to caution, not overloaded with fear.

Here's how.

It's all about preparation and visualization of what it takes to operate outside your comfort zone. It's also a relentless commitment to self-awareness and instinct that abounds within the survivors, along with a vulnerability to share with others their internal frustrations, fears, and failures.

Here are your steps.

Get prepared.

While the unknown often equals fear, preparedness equals confidence. When you are confident, you, in turn, experience less fear because you have uncovered something previously unknown to you. Take, for example, the concept of caregiving for a parent. I couldn't begin to tell you how many people have told me about feeling "stuck" in their situation of needing to care for an aging parent. They love their parents dearly. But they also have lives filled with other people and tasks requiring their attention. Children of their own. Jobs. Friends. Neighbors. Communities.

The added need to care for Mom or Dad can lead to depletion. It's a cost that grown children may sincerely want to pay, but it can come with little to no warning, and nobody prepared for it. Maybe nobody has the resources. Or, nobody thought to have the financial conversations about lifestyle costs and sacrifices until it became impossible because of mental incapacity. (In other words, everyone waited too long to talk about tough stuff.) And let's not even mention the resentment of planning for your own long-term care when your parents didn't. Layer in some self-imposed guilt or complex family dynamics, and you can imagine the outcome.

Unforeseen expenses like caring for an aging parent may feel as foreign to you as the dot-com bubble burst did to us financial advisors back in 2001. But just as we learned that corrections are a normal part of the market, we also know that even "unforeseen" expenses are foreseeable, and we've helped figure out ways you can prepare for them—even if your parent isn't willing.

This is just one example of how you can prepare even when you think you can't. And that preparedness can be financial, emotional, or both. There are many more examples.

Visualize what you want.

So, let's return to the idea that you may very well experience at least one major unforeseen expense before life is over. Think *now* how you want to feel in that moment, when that level of change walks through your door. What do you want to have in place? What will allow you to stay in the mindset of caution and not cross over into fear? Maybe there are some changes to make in your life today in order to set yourself up for success on that day. Take a little time to settle into the imaginative mind, and let yourself be the person faced with a big hurdle. Who does the you in your mind need beside her to conquer that? What needs to be present in your life to equip you for a smooth transition beyond the change?

Reaching beyond your comfort zone can be difficult if you don't truly feel you belong there. That's where visualization comes into play. Brain studies reveal that thoughts produce the exact same mental instructions as actions (Ho 2019). So, training your brain to visualize your future helps you begin to plan for today.

Share your fears.

You can break these fearful, negative feelings by sharing your thoughts with others. Nine times out of ten, you'll see you are not alone. Find someone you trust and allow yourself to share your reservations with them. Invite that person to do the same with you in return. Fear can cause you to feel so much shame and self-doubt that you imagine all your friends and family laughing at you. Fortunately, most people's fear-based thoughts are not original. Many people you know feel the same way but won't share. Like you, they may fear appearing weak or unintelligent. If you have second-guessed your abilities or have been afraid to take a chance when you know you deserve better, know that many others have felt this way, too.

The more you expose your fears, the more you learn that fear does not belong explicitly to you. The fears could lessen once you put them into a proper context.

It sure helped me having a few close advisor friends during that first major market breakdown at the tender age of 33. And it sure helps today because, out of that shared experience, we became better people. We are better navigators as survivors. We grew immensely and didn't even see it at the time. The icing on the fear cake is that when you can push through some of these mental barriers, you have much more confidence and a mountain of stories for others who may travel that path.

16

Shift Toward Goals Worth Getting

"Goals allow you to control the direction of change in your favor."

Brian Tracy

Prior to whatever change in your life sparked this book's presence therein, what were your goals? Your dreams? Did you achieve them?

Do you still want to?

I'm going to guess you've seen at least one football game in your life and that you know the process of play is to move the ball down the field toward the opponent's end zone. The team is given four tries (downs) to get ten yards closer to that goal. If they do so, they get another four tries.

Narrator: You do realize that thousands of people watch this game, right?

Of course I do. Stay with me.

The team goes into the first down with a play in mind

that is supposed to land them at a specific place on the field. Now, how many times have you seen a quarterback throw a pass, only to see the ball go sailing over or past the intended receiver?

Assuming they are able to recover from the failed pass and didn't lose possession, the team must make a decision: try that play again—or switch to a new way. Often, they quickly settle on a new strategy for getting those ten yards. The team reassembles at the line of scrimmage and tries out a new play for achieving the goal.

All humans share the same general life goal—the same end zone, so to speak. We're all trying to get to an enjoyable life experience. How we define "enjoyable" is different for each of us, of course. Mother Theresa found it most enjoyable to pour her life into others in service. Amelia Earhart defined "enjoyable" as constantly being able to fly airplanes. It's probably safe to say that Taylor Swift finds it enjoyable to write and perform songs. Jane Goodall enjoys protecting animals and their habitats.

As I said, "an enjoyable life" means different things to different people.

It can even mean different things in different phases of life.

I'll never forget the discussion I had with a client one time regarding her retirement. Together, we'd created a plan, and she'd carefully followed it for years. When she achieved the financial goal she'd set, she retired.

And then, sitting in my office, she asked me, "Is this all there is?"

She'd worked very hard for a long time, diligently earning yard after yard toward the end zone of retirement.

And she'd done it. She got there! But, after spiking the ball and doing the victory dance and receiving the slaps on the back for winning, she wasn't quite sure what to do with herself or her resources.

Did you know Vera Wang did not start out as a fashion designer? She began as a pairs figure skater. As a teenager, she and her partner made it all the way to the 1968 U. S. Figure Skating Championships—but their fifth-place finish didn't qualify for the Olympics. So, Ms. Wang re-defined her "enjoyable" and began designing. Her work received international attention when she designed Nancy Kerrigan's outfits for both the 1992 and 1994 Olympics. In 2009, Ms. Wang was inducted into the U. S. Figure Skating Hall of Fame—not for her skating, but for her contributions to the sport *as a costume designer*.

You have complete and total permission to define "enjoyable" for yourself *now*. That may have absolutely nothing in common with how you defined "enjoyable" in previous years, or it could be similar, but different. Or, like a football team, you may need to huddle and rethink the plays it will take to get you to the same end zone.

Here is an exercise to get you started toward pursuing goals. Before setting them, we need to take a hard look at the end zone—the definition of "enjoyable life"—you had before Change entered the picture. Allow yourself to sit fully into this new phase of life as you answer the following questions:

1. What, if any, goals did I hold before this change came?
2. Do these goals align with whom I am now?

3. How would it feel today to set those old goals aside?
4. How would it feel a year from now to have set those goals aside today?
5. Is there a goal that I think is too lofty and if so, why?
6. What would it take to actually accomplish a lofty goal?
7. What would be a "second-best" effort in that area that was good but just not so lofty?
8. How would I feel if I accomplished the second-best goal rather than the original one?
9. What is holding me back from outlining or accomplishing new goals?
10. What are my personal limitations?
11. What could I do to overcome my personal limitations?
12. Are there things in my life that might block or lessen the ability to reach my goals?
13. Am I willing to address what blocks me at least partially if not completely?
14. Am I willing to compromise on a goal?
15. What does a successful, well-lived life look like today?
16. What will a successful, well-lived life look like at the end of my life?

Once you've taken some good time to sit with the answers to these, perhaps it is an ideal time to remind ourselves of the 5/25 rule that Warren Buffet is famous for using. His approach is to come up with 25 goals and narrow those to just your top five. By saying NO to the bottom twenty of them, you end up focusing on what truly matters most to you. Of course, this isn't exactly for everyone because some people would just come up with twenty things they don't care about just to cross them off. My point is that with goals, fewer is better, and this exercise will help you decide what's truly important. I'd call these an "enjoyable life" list. And I'd take these focii into our next few chapters!

17

Realize It is Not All About the Benjamins

"There is a gigantic difference between earning money and being rich."

Marlene Dietrich

Today, the action we'll take is that of a mind shift. At the beginning of this book, I mentioned that regardless of how much you have, money helps you across the abyss of change only partially at best. Accumulating enough to retire comfortably might be only one part of an enjoyable life. Even some of the best financial advisors don't address the critical thing needed to live a successful life: meaning.

And you're not going to find that in money.

No matter what anyone believes or tells you, money doesn't bring your life meaning. Having money doesn't hurt because it certainly provides options, but it will *always* fail to provide meaning. Money itself is not a goal, though it can be fuel that takes you to your goal.

For instance, let's say an enjoyable life for you is fully owning two properties: a main residence and one large enough for the extended family to join you on vacation. So, your goal is set. You will need money to achieve that goal. You'll *also* need *discernment* to make your way toward the ideal property and the most advantageous deal on it. You'll need *communication skills* to navigate new relationships with realtors and/or property owners. You'll need *curiosity* as you seek out places in the new location to meet your basic need for groceries, electricity, water, and waste management. You'll need *patience* as the inevitable unforeseen challenges arise throughout the process.

See how money isn't the only tool you need to build this dream? Discernment, communication skills, curiosity, and patience often require dedicated attention to cultivate and strengthen. If all you bring to this goal is money, you could very well waste it.

So, when you progress in this book to the chapters on Vision and Mission, try to avoid setting any that are solely about money. "I will have $7 million in the bank by age sixty" is not as useful as, "I will own a home in Florida, pay for my child's college education, and be able to take at least one meaningful trip each year." These are worthy missions if they align with your vision of yourself. We can then look at the costs of completing those missions for the dollar figure that serves as one of the tools you'll need.

Don't forget to reflect on what is going on in your family, the circles in which you operate, and the world. Are you passionate about any causes that a few Benjamins could fuel? Do you feel strongly about any problems that your talents or resources could solve?

So many of the things we enjoy cost money. Let's take the arts as an example. Who knew that a baritone saxophone costs around $7,000–8,000 and that the average person playing in a symphony doesn't even own their instrument? High-quality music requires more than ticket sales, especially if the performers don't have record deals. Maybe if you are blessed with a solid financial picture, you could give to your local symphony.

This is just one example of where you might direct some of your time and talents to make life better, more enjoyable for others. Consider causes or interests that are:

- Social
- Financial
- Relational
- Educational
- Career-driven
- Parental-driven
- Spiritual
- Business-wise
- Health-wise

If you have something in mind, how can you contribute, financially and/or otherwise?

Before we move on, I'd like you to name two of the big accomplishments we compiled back on Day 13. List them here:

Now, for each of the things you've listed, name all the things *other than money* that you needed to accomplish those milestones:

Celebrate these. Use them as inspiration. And be grateful to know that money is not the crucial factor. It's one thing in a list of many. Keep that in mind as we move forward together tomorrow.

18

Assess Your Financial Resources

"The goal isn't more money. The goal is living life on your terms."

Will Rogers

A s we've concluded, money isn't everything, but it is something. For most of us, that something is security and options. Whatever plans you made or didn't, change has brought you the chance to begin anew. That beginning may have additional financial challenges or include opportunities now or in the future. Taking an inventory of where you are and where you want to be is critical before you begin identifying your new Vision and Mission.

To begin this process, consider the answers to the following six questions with dollar amounts and dates related to your current assets, savings, and spending:

1. What assets do I have in retirement accounts (401K, IRAs, Roth IRAs, deferred compensation, or annuities)? And what amount do I have in non-retirement accounts and more liquid, accessible investments (joint/individual accounts in stock, mutual funds, CDs, bank)
2. How much am I saving and where am I investing those savings?
3. What financial obligations (short or long-term) do I have that require a lump sum payment outside my regular lifestyle/budget?
4. Do I have any new financial obligations which don't require a lump sum but do add materially to my monthly standard of living?
5. Are there significant additional assets or income where money is no longer a concern and if so, do you have a picture of the rate of increase in net worth over time?
6. Are any financial obligations going away in the coming years?

Once you get a handle on the big picture of your finances, it becomes helpful to construct a detailed financial statement of your current position. This should concisely list your liquid assets, retirement assets, liabilities (debts), and net worth (the assets minus the debts). Having this snapshot view of your resources is also beneficial for your planning or if you visit with a professional advisor.

Next, it's often important to understand how you spend money depending on the stage you are in financially. Some people take the approach of writing down everything they can think of monthly and its cost. Inevitably, you spend a lot of time and still leave things out. Instead, I suggest reviewing your banking balances over a six-to-twelve-month period. If your balance remains unchanged, you can assume you are spending what you make. If it's higher, you can probably afford to save more—or give more. If it's lower, you likely need to re-look at your budget. Looking at cash flow this way seems to save time and help people arrive at a baseline assumption of what income they need to live and how much flexibility exists.

These exercises are important regardless of your age and stage. If you have a larger portfolio or have reached your financial goals, then working with an advisor can help you create more choices for your life and money. If not—well, you cannot fight math, but a financial advisor can help you make the choices you need to improve the math.

19

Catch a Vision

"Where there is no vision, the people perish..."

Proverbs 29:18

It's Vision Day! When you've gone through a significant change, it can be challenging to let yourself think about what you truly want *for yourself*—especially if that change is impacting people you care about. Your inclination may be to set aside anything for yourself and instead rush to soothe the hurts they're experiencing from the change. And that's okay, of course, for a while.

But it is neither healthy nor sustainable to soothe others as you neglect yourself entirely. So here, in this chapter, I invite you to gently set aside your concerns for others and use this time to get acquainted with your own desires as you identify your Vision for your life.

Your Vision concerns your future. Where are you going? What do you want your life to be about and for? Maybe you had answers to those questions before the change came into your life that prompted you to pick up this book. If you did, are your answers the same? It's okay to fine-tune them—even change them entirely. It's your life. You have total freedom to stay the course or change things up.

What you'll work on today is not about pleasing others unless your Vision for your life is to have pleased everyone around you. (And if you figure out how to do that, you'll definitely need a financial manager for all the money you're about to make in having done the impossible!)

Quick note: Your Vision is not to be confused with your Mission, which we'll get into in the next chapter.

Today, I want you to think about your future. What do you aspire to be from this point forward? Why? What matters to you? What lights you up? What excites you? What hits you with a feeling of dread? (That's often an indicator that it isn't for you.)

Picture yourself as a hundred-year-old woman ready to close your eyes for the final time. What's on your mind? Who (if anyone) is physically with you? Where are you? What are people saying when they hear of your passing? The answers to these questions can reveal important information as you think about writing your own Vision Statement.

Examples of a Personal Vision Statement include:

- Use the power of story to usher in healing and hope.
- Give of my talents and skills in a way that benefits my family and community both now and in the future.
- Seek adventure while leaving kindness in my wake as I move with curiosity throughout the world.

- Raise up a family that is connected and loving toward me and each other, generation after generation.
- Make drug addiction a problem of the past and influence the community impacted by it in a substantial way.
- Build a business and home that inspire and serve others toward life-giving ends.
- Be physically healthy and inspire positive change for those who struggle with self-image.

Notice these Vision Statements are forward-thinking and somewhat broad. By reading them, though, did you immediately get a sense for what this person is about?

Let's take a look at that last one—more or less, "to better the physical health of myself and others." You'll find a myriad of ways to achieve this. Become a medical doctor. Learn herbal medicine. Rid the world of a toxin or two. Create a restaurant that only serves organic, sustainably raised food. Make sustainable agriculture available in all cities so produce retains more nutrients from farm to table. You can probably think of others.

By keeping your Vision somewhat broad, you allow room to flesh out the details of achieving it. (We'll get into this more in the next chapter.)

The key here is to be both broad in statement and yet specific in values. I know, I know. That sounds somewhat paradoxical. Take a look at that last example again, though. Notice that the person didn't say, "To better the health of people." That is so broad as to say nearly nothing. What kind of health? Spiritual? Mental? Physical? Something else?

Note the qualifiers: "Be *physically* healthy and inspire positive change *for those who struggle with self-image*." These help to provide more direction. This person is clearly about doing her part to make bodies and minds work better—both hers and others. And this specificity in her Vision Statement serves as the lens through which she can view the opportunities life presents and determine if they are hers.

Some Vision Statements are meant to be attainable daily. Others are meant to outline the best possible state that would occur if all things went right. Both or either work. "A world without Alzheimer's" is a pretty ambitious vision, yet the Alzheimer's Association has no hesitation about what they see as "success" for their organization. So it should be with your vision statement. Attainable and yet aspirational.

Today's exercise is your chance to project what you believe is "success" or "fulfillment" of the time you spend on this big earth of ours. Odds are that you aren't able to fully articulate a vision in a single exercise or day. You can start, however. Let's go back to the hundred-year-old woman—YOU—we alluded to earlier in the chapter. Here are a few things to think about ...

- Given your biggest strengths, what words come to mind in the context of being fulfilled? Successful?
- What things really fueled your fire or made you most excited in your best days? Why?
- What do/did you do better or uniquely differently than others that is a big deal (even if you don't talk about it or get credit for it)?

- No matter what you happen to be doing, is it more in your nature to do things or exhibit certain behaviors? (In other words, are you a "do-er" or a "be-er"?) One is more about the process, and the other is more outcome oriented.
  - For the Do-ers: What are the people, problems, and projects that mean the most to you? If you were able to tackle one of those and/or make a positive change there, what would that look like?
  - For the Be-ers: What are some of the most important qualities or values to you? If you used those to their fullest extent, what would happen?

Given the change you just experienced, what possible improvement to your life's purpose or vision could you realize? Wrap all that together in your head and take a shot at writing down a vision statement of your own using these guidelines. You also might try to do some quick research on company vision statements. They may provide some inspiration to help you perfect your own personal one.

We want that hundred-year-old you to be smiling... and fulfilled. The Vision Statement is one thing you can use as a touchpoint toward success as you step into this next chapter of living.

20

Your Mission, Should You Choose to Accept It

"Vision sees the stars; mission carves the path to reach them."

Aloo Denish Obiero

It's Mission Statement Day! I love Mission Statements because they make my action-oriented brain happy. They are the vehicles that, if accomplished, eventually achieve the Vision you wrote in the previous chapter. They also change as you complete them and move through life.

Mission is huge! HUGE! And change has a way of helping you crystallize your mission. It has a way of burning away the distractions and distilling you down to action that truly matters to you. You can feel strongly about things and yet the bigger the change, the more clear your current path comes into focus.

I was lucky. I feel like I got plopped right into a place where career mission really ended up being a bleed-over to a personal mission. Two for one. It may sound odd, but I think my mission chose me. And I'm so grateful for it. From the beginning of my career, I never felt my job was to do financial planning or wealth management. It was my duty every day to help others get to a point in their lives where they could make the choice to do anything—and from that freedom they could then find their personal way to contribute.

What *did* change was a tweak in my company mission as a result of two divorces, career alignment choices, and attaining my own financial freedom. I'd learned a ton, yet life was still empty in some key ways for me. It forced a mission evolution. A refinement. A deeper focus on the original. No longer was my old purpose good enough.

Originally, I began my career to "distinctively serve clients for the lifetime of their families." This meant being ahead of the pack, on the forefront of financial planning and innovation. While noble, still, my original mission needed to deepen for me to feel that my contribution was at its highest. I want to be that hundred-year-old with a BIG smile and lots of memories and accomplishments. Now, the mission has broadened to include helping others toward success, fulfillment, and giving back in tangible ways.

Before we get to your exercise in mission writing, here are a few examples of mission statements from others:

- To use my parenting skills to raise emotionally balanced and confident children.
- To speak into others' lives in a way that inspires them to do good.

- Teaching students about becoming all they can be inside and outside the classroom.
- Welcome and serve those struggling with addiction so that they are equipped to re-enter general society as productive citizens.
- Bring culture-enriching stories into mass media channels.
- To help others manage their financial resources to achieve their identified, life-enriching goals.

It doesn't have to be elaborate. The job of the Mission Statement is to be a grounding tool. In fact, it can be short actions toward living what you deem a successful life (to which you gave voice via your Vision Statement). Start with the results of yesterday's exercise. Define that future state—and work backwards to get your mission clarified.

- Why do you think you were put here, given all you've experienced?
- What are the one or two activities (or values) that you would like to claim as your personal contribution for having lived a good and meaningful life?

Life has a way of sometimes getting us away from our true purpose. We can get caught up in the things we have to do and miss the things we are meant to do. Mission is all about what you do that is purposeful and meaningful. It's what can bring you great joy. And it's especially worth reflecting on after experiencing change because you are a different and better you. Don't waste the opportunity.

21

To Hire, Or Not to Hire

"If you think it's expensive to hire a professional, wait until you hire an amateur."

Red Adair

A number of readers of this book may revisit their financial picture as a result of the change they experience. Change has an uncanny way of pushing people to evaluate their whole life, and finances are often a big part of that. People who have subscribed to a do-it-yourself approach for years, or even worked with an advisor or two, get hit with change and think, "What do I do now?"

The re-evaluation process is a great time to think about Marshall Goldsmith's *What Got You Here Won't Get You There.* How you managed your finances prior to this change might have landed you in a good place, but that doesn't matter. The question of today is: Will that method get you the rest of the way in the manner you need? Or is there a different way that fits you better now?

A quick caveat before we go on: All financial advisors are not created equal. We can work in different business models and pay structures, with different philosophies and processes around how we invest or plan. We may even specialize in a specific circumstance (e.g. tax planning, estate planning, inheritance, divorce, etc.) or client group (e.g. doctors, engineers, GenX, Boomers, etc.). We may work at banks, wirehouses, insurance companies, or independently. And an "independent" advisor, confusingly enough, can be fully independent or underneath/aligned with another corporate partner. We can have industry designations (letters after our signature lines) which may look the same yet probably point to a wide variety of levels of training. It can be hard to understand if you're not really that familiar with the industry.

In an effort to help you navigate that confusion and identify a financial advisor who can truly assist you at this point in your life, I've put together some questions to ask potential advisors. I don't mean it to be an exhaustive study of every angle, only a helpful way to launch your next chapter in the most effective way possible. It is also not meant to disparage other great advisors. It simply is my own suggestion to help you get information out of the advisor which they may not share up front so you can align that with how you feel about life and money.

1. Do you have a defined investment process? If so, how did you come about adopting that process?

You want to find out whether there is a methodology to how an advisor would invest your money. If there is, that framework can lend itself to more consistent results over time due to a common rationale for decision making. You might ask for examples of how that process has played out both good and bad.

Asking about the evolution of any process or how they work today versus yesterday might give you some good information as well. Maybe the advisor changed firms and processes or systems were a part of that. Their career history certainly is relevant. It's not that one way is the exact right way, but if you don't explore this question, you might never know the wide variety of philosophies or approaches. One day you could find yourself misaligned and shopping for a new advisor.

Do they construct their own portfolios or act somewhat as a re-seller of others' ideas? What do they believe to be the advantages or disadvantages of their choice to do that? If they are affiliated with a firm, does that have anything to do with the process?

The conversation you have around this subject helps you uncover certain traits and values of that advisor which may help you feel more aligned with one person or another. You may really want someone who has a more structured process whereas others might want someone who adopts a more flexible framework. It's not that one is right or wrong; it's the one that aligns more with you.

2. In your opinion, is there a difference between financial planning and wealth management? How would that apply or play out in my situation?

This is intentionally a loaded question. Their answer should reveal the responder's view of what financial planning really encompasses. Can they explain it on the back of a napkin or do they illustrate it with slick charts and graphs? Or is it more of an interactive, living process? What part of their method seems cookie-cutter, and how much is customized? (Complete/holistic approaches are generally going to cost more. Definitions of holistic may be different from advisor to advisor.) All of this is good to know and understand.

As is how much planning the advisor believes is beneficial for someone in your exact circumstances or with your level of assets. Why pay for something you don't need, right? On the other hand, if you value a more holistic approach, then the potential extra cost is worth it. Either way, the question above will help you decide.

Full disclosure: I tend to take a holistic approach to financial advising. This is because I think the biggest weakness in the financial industry today is the lack of attention to addressing the complete picture of one's success. We advisors tend to address retirement, education planning, or tax planning, and things of that nature. We help people set goals and achieve financial milestones. And we call that "success."

Yet it's the very change you've just experienced that whispers, "You know, it's more than money. We've been through this experience now and have this new-found knowledge. Let's use it."

This thought process of meeting financial goals—and adding the dimension of a fulfillment factor—points to a whole new level of conversations and approach. We as an industry are feeling our way through it, and some (including me) are committed to engaging with clients at deeper levels. I cannot help but think that the anticipated $124 trillion of assets projected to change hands between 2024 and 2048 (Cerulli[3]) will encourage our industry to push for different conversations and more holistic service offerings. In that same 24-year period, 43% of that $124 trillion is projected to pass to a surviving spouse—with more than 95% of that wealth going to women (*USA Today*[4]).

Those statistics point to the increasing need for a more whole-person, whole-life approach well before one spouse dies. Studies indicate men and women think differently about money and investing. This is especially needed by wives who did not grow up in a culture of understanding and managing assets themselves. In my opinion, the coming massive changeover of asset ownership also creates an opportunity for the lead child (who may be the executor or successor trustee) to step up and join the planning. If there are more commas and zeros at stake, a financial planning or wealth management relationship

---

[3] *Cerulli A Changing Financial Advice Industry: Key Trends in 2025* https://publications.investmentsandwealth.org/iwpublications/library/item/january_february_2025/4254117

[4] *USA Today* https://www.usatoday.com/story/money/2025/05/20/american-women-inherit-50-million-great-wealth-transfer/83722460007/

should go beyond just a financial target. It should even go beyond holistic. It should go to the level of fulfillment.

That's why I think the exercise of Chapter 19 is so important. Your view of success probably will encompass so much more than a figure on an investment statement. And you should embrace and amplify that, given you'll likely have more than enough to live on. Which should lead you to ask: what do you do with excess wealth? If this is your question, you should be sure your advisor is on the forefront of change and capability.

3. How would you describe the average client that you serve?

You want to understand whether the advisor considers you a small or large client (based on asset levels and financial planning circumstances) compared to their normal client. If you are small, then you run the risk of getting ignored. If you are small but are likely to become an inheritor, then that's fine—maybe even ideal—but make sure you get served! If the advisor considers you a large client, then at the risk of sounding crass, you don't want to be the lab rat on which they experiment.

Likewise, it's helpful to see yourself and your circumstances as a part of what an advisor has a propensity to do well—over and over. This connects that to the consistency of results. If he or she supports others like you well, you will likely be happy with the relationship long term.

22

Final Words

"Champions keep playing until they get it right."

Billie Jean King

You know, this next generation may not know much about Billie Jean. I didn't. Without a doubt, Billie Jean King survived and overcame a ton of opposition and change. In her time, women were only a speck on the sports radar, especially from an income standpoint. Directly from her biography, Billy Jean was one of nine players who broke away from the tennis establishment and accepted one-dollar contracts from tennis promoter Gladys Heldman in Houston—all of which led to the birth of women's professional tennis. Here are a few of her firsts:

- **1971:** First female athlete in any sport to earn more than $100,000 in prize money.
- **1972:** First woman to be chosen *Sports Illustrated* "Sportsperson of the Year."

- **1973:** First person to win the U. S. Open under new rules awarding equal prize money for men and women. It would take another 34 years for all four major tournaments to do the same.
- **1973:** First to found two organizations solely dedicated to promote women in sports (the Women's Tennis Association and then later the Women's Sports Foundation).
- **1973:** Won the first female-male competitive tennis match, the Battle of the Sexes. Watched by millions, this milestone stood as a bold illustration of the capability of women in a male-dominated field and supported her plight for equal compensation.
- **1974:** First woman to coach a co-ed team in professional sports (Philadelphia Freedoms, World Table Tennis)
- **1984:** First woman commissioner in professional sports history (World Team Tennis)

Years later, *LIFE Magazine* named her one of the "100 Most Important Americans of the 20th Century" (1990) and *Sports Illustrated* named her one of the Greatest Athletes of the Century (1999).

Meanwhile, as a young pup completely unaware of all the political or social change stuff out there surrounding her, I watched her on the tennis court. I also remember the entry of the next huge female tennis star, Chrissie Evert. My parents apparently liked to watch a lot of tennis. Somehow the ultimate "girl next door," she was the more adored version of Billie Jean King on the courts and didn't suffer the barriers of her predecessor.

Chris Evert is known for her 18 Grand Slam singles titles and a 125-match winning streak on clay courts. She was a key person in the early years of the Women's Tennis Association and has been involved in several charitable endeavors, but just wasn't as vocal about social change as Billy Jean. While playing a significant role, Chris furthered the growth of the sport for women but likely wouldn't be categorized as an activist for change.

At the 2025 US Open when Chris was honored on her 50th anniversary of her 1975 winning title, Chris said that "life didn't start until after I retired." Astonishing! All that success on the tennis court, and yet what she talked about when "life started"—raising three children and the mantra of "encouraging little girls all over the world that they can do anything". Billy Jean said it was her "authenticity" whether that's on the court or along her journey with ovarian cancer which drew people to her and to the sport of tennis. Chris seems to have found what's important to her. The cancer journey helped to "open her eyes to love and friendship" even more.

Both of these women are fierce competitors and thus are cut from a different cloth. Their lives and visions of what they wanted their careers to accomplish were different. The way they went about living out their passion was very different. And yet, I think they have a message to us all: KEEP PLAYING!

No one can truly understand the unique nature of your experience.

No one can walk through the valley and experience life the way you have with your change when it was at its worst part.

No one can benefit from the choices you made and the wisdom you gained—unless you share it.

There is no denying that change can be a debilitating experience. Or that it can provide you with a unique opportunity to energize yourself and make a unique contribution within your circle, your community, or the world.

You have the tools. God, in whatever form you understand (Him / Her/ That/ Them/ Whatever), gifted you with that when you were created. These tools have been honed over your years, and change gives you the option to hone them further—and more quickly and sharply.

You can have a vision, and you must re-make yourself.

The job is yours. To the extent you take this on and incorporate into your fabric, you can make the launch of your next chapter more successful.

Keep in mind, even the professionals will hit the ball out and fail to clear the net on the best shot they thought they'd make on the tennis court. Life accommodates, and continues, for us all.

Just. Keep. Playing.

Acknowledgments

I would not be standing atop this "author" mountain speaking effectively to you about change without the blessing of many, many people and organizations who fed their wisdom into me during the journey.

Thank you to my true father, Rob Moxley. Although the references in this book are not always direct, the influence you had on my life is irreplaceable. You are God's gift to me every day. You saved me, inspired me, endured me, and most of all, you loved me no matter what. No child believed you more than I did when you told me I could do anything. And because of your wisdom, the words in every chapter of the book and my life are imprinted with your DNA. You are an extraordinary person and the foundation that you laid as a father to me is a strong inspiration behind this book, which could very well affect lives after we both no longer walk this earth. You are a powerful example to all fathers and all people.

And my immeasurable gratitude goes to my mother, Lydia Moxley. We are quite different in many respects, yet our core is so aligned. Your influence over me especially in my early years—taking the high road when Larry failed, working diligently to raise a daughter with values you held dear, and reinforcing that I was loved by an alcoholic father in his weakness—has paid off in spades. You made lemonade out of lemons naturally, and you pushed me to do something of value in the world. This I carry today to my clients as they reach their goals and press beyond them.

Thank you to my current team at Investor's Resource—Martha Gilpin, Chandra Hudson, Matt Leahy, Dale Hubbert, Brock Eson, and Lara Brown—for upholding our mission of distinctively serving clients. We've trailblazed a lot over the years and walked through a ton of storms and change, which is rarely a comfortable situation. It means the world to me that you moved "with me" and adapted—especially as this book began to transform from a simple gift to clients going through loss into something that would reach a larger circle. Thank you for accompanying me into the unknown with faith that something good will happen.

There are no appropriate words to describe my appreciation and indebtedness to the two women, Dwaynia and Rebeca, who helped me physically write this book. Dwaynia Wilkerson tirelessly revised time after time while concepts were forming and ideas were gelling. Thank you for not firing me as a client on Round 2 when I confessed that I couldn't put my name on the Round 1 version of the book despite massive rewrites. You were there when I said I wanted to write a book but had no idea what that would look like. You were instrumental to get the creative juices flowing and organizing chaos!

Thank you to Nancy Iannitteli, who I met getting a haircut on one of my first stays as a part-time resident in

Naples, FL. I told her about the book, and she floated the idea of meeting a local publisher. From there, the entire book concept transformed. It's almost as if the world opened up and widened. We have yet to see how many lives may be touched by this work; but it is for sure that it would not have happened in this way, shape, or form without her gentle words of introduction. It makes you think about the small things you do in a day. They make a difference. Hers sure did.

Rebeca Seitz, through Rebeca Books as my publisher, will likely go down as one of the top people in a lifetime that changed my trajectory. Meeting her through Nancy was nothing short of a God-moment. She may not have needed me; but I needed her. She has gifted me with an enormous amount of time and energy. She poured into me as someone who wanted to help humanity and perhaps, through this work, we may just do that! It was her insight and experience that convinced me to change the focus and target of the book. After 2+ years of writing, that was the last thing I wanted to do. Yet her words both killed and inspired me: "This is a really good book if you self-publish... but if you want it to go beyond some gifts to people you know and meet, it needs to be rewritten." She took me from a point of having nothing left to say or write and press-on to re-write this book, with professional help, one more time. She encouraged me to have the patience until she had room in her publishing line to take me on as an author—while letting me "go" and seek other publishers if that was my choice. This book is better than I could ever have done myself. Keen patience and wisdom...I am completely beyond words in appreciation.

To Jayne Hollum, thank you for being close to me and supporting me in whatever I do. Your love and friendship are fuel to my fire. Your heart is bigger than anything. The longer I live, the more I know this is the essence of living.

To Kathy Ellis, thank you for having the same "screw loose" and celebrating that in your daily living! You are a gift to your clients, your family, and so many others. I'm lucky to call you friend and am so appreciative you were one of the few women in the room in this traditionally male-dominated field we find ourselves thriving in today!

Thank you to my former husbands, Bo Lovell and Jamie Burnum. We loved and we experienced so much together. Thank you for being in my life for whatever period that was or is and for what you contributed to our marriage and friendship. I wish the world for you.

To Hal Jones, my special friend, thank you for the time you've invested with me and for caring and supporting me throughout the whole process of this book. Some days, I needed more and you were certainly there.

To my former father-in-law, Jim Lovell (deceased), for saving me early in my career and giving me a salary to get my own business going by answering telephones for his insurance business part-time. My original first real mentor, Jim allowed a young woman who loved financial planning, but who wasn't the best at "selling", to survive. Without him, I wouldn't be in this career or writing this book.

Thank you to Charlotte Baldwin, my counselor through both divorces. You taught me another dimension of God's love and brought resources to me for wisdom and discernment. I may still be crazy, but I'm more at peace, settled, and an excellent processor-of-information because of the years we spent together. Many of the concepts in this book were derived from the counseling foundation that you laid out and the hard work you encouraged me to do.

As long as we are looking back, a big thank you goes to Birmingham Southern College, the Business and English Departments, and so many relationships which were formed decades ago. Long live liberal arts in conjunction with business education. The education there was foundational. The friendships stirred my heart and seeing the success of each of you confirms we all have a role and purpose—as changing as that might be through the years.

On the subject of college buddies, thank you to Leslie Miller and Louise Randolph. You lived with me, which cannot be easy! We didn't know at the time how much our experiences would set up the road for future success. You were kind and open—and my first experiences and memories without Mom and Dad were formed with you. It may sound corny, but you marked a place in my life that I may not have acknowledged the importance of until this book. People have an effect if they are there long enough. We talked to all hours of the night and shared our closest thoughts. This was a treasure—is a treasure—and I'm thankful for you.

Another big thank you to Vestavia High School teachers—and especially to Randy Faust, my cross country and track coach—" SET GO!" I remember that saying today when I think of beginning a project. I'll try hard not to remember: "Moxley, my grandmother can run faster than you backwards... let's go." Thank you to so many other teachers and coaches, for your influence over impressionable young people to keep them working hard and reaching the next goal.

To Chris Cockfield, Susan Doughty, and Andrea Moore. You were my first stable girlfriends in high school for a period longer than a few years. Today you are beautiful people and helped me in my formative years weather the high school storms and prepare for the big steps of college.

Finally, to all my clients over the years, please know that serving you has given me such personal fulfillment! YOU are the impetus of this book because as I've grown older and more experienced in this business, I realize that you have allowed me the gift to serve multiple roles in the life of your family. And since I can't clone myself or ask the good Lord to give us all more than 24 hours in a day, I wanted a guide to allow you to experience more peace, confidence, or fulfillment no matter what comes your way in life. My hope is this book can be just that as well as a means for you to extend that opportunity to those who mean the most to you. Thank you for your trust and confidence in my team and me to allow us into your lives. You are my family.

To think that a book of this nature could touch lives of individuals whom I will never personally meet seems like an awfully big aspiration. And yet, why put a limit on what is possible? Thank you to the people who take the time to read and reflect on life. I truly believe you can be used in ways that are far beyond any of our human comprehension. And that possibility excites me more than you could ever know. I wonder how many new paths I will cross and, if ours should, I welcome the conversation.